THE LAST BEST DAY

A TROUT FISHER'S PERSPECTIVE

— BY —

MICHAEL ALTIZER

WITH ETCHINGS BY

BRETT SMITH

PUBLISHED BY
SPORTING CLASSICS

THE LAST BEST DAY -
A TROUT FISHER'S PERSPECTIVE
is published by Sporting Classics
Columbia, South Carolina
www.sportingclassics.com
800-849-1004

Publisher & Editor: Chuck Wechsler

Cover & Inside Art: Brett Smith

Printed in the United States.

Second Edition

Library of Congress Control Number: 2007931638

ISBN 0-9778551-5-5
978-0-9778551-5-5

For Carly and Jane,
without whom I would be absent.

For Beth, Alan and Jack,
beloved sister and brothers,
fly fishers all.

And for Chuck Wechsler,
my editor, my mentor
and my friend.

———————————

But most of all for my Mother,
Tommy Helen Cruey Altizer
who nearly caught the first
trout I remember.

And for my Dad,
Claude Charles Altizer
… who did.

VI

• ACKNOWLEDGEMENTS & THANKS •

– From the End of a Long Dirt Road –

A friend full of wisdom once told me that everything good in life sits at the end of a dirt road. At the time, we were overlooking the St. Johns River in Florida and had just finished the best catfish dinner I've ever had at a great little restaurant that sits by the water at the end of just such a dirt road. If what he says is true, and I do believe it is, then there are many people whose tracks overlay my own along the road that has led to this book.

First and foremost, I wish to express my deepest appreciation and respect to Chuck Wechsler, who first saw fit to loose these stories on the world. Chuck and I have poked our noses into the wind from the longleaf pines of southern Georgia to the high country of northern New Mexico, and our paths together still stretch ahead of us into the great unknown.

I have always been an admirer of Brett Smith, but it wasn't until I saw his fly-fishing etchings that I realized what a truly great artist he is. Brett's etchings and cover painting have made this book far richer than it might otherwise have been.

My undying gratitude goes to Flip and Diane Pallot. Diane and I share a language of purpose that I have with no one else. And though Flip and I have never actually fished together, he has been one of my most treasured guides through this life for many years. His advice, encouragement, laughter, generosity, and most importantly his friendship mean more to me than I can adequately express.

There are other guides with whom I have been privileged to share many rich days. Among the finest are Frank Simms, Pat Carpenter, Jaime Ortiz, Terry Tiner, Al Ward, Matthew Hynes, Josh Young, Andrew Bennett, Ed Ward, Sandy Moret, Diana Rudolf, Clyde Douglass, Todd Rogers, Chuck Turner, Randy Hickman and Matt Dollar, a fascinating cast of characters who I have followed into some of the most sublime places in my experience.

VIII

Verlin Altizer and his son David go back farther than my memory can reach. And though David and I are now left here without our Dads, they still are and evermore shall be our most important and cherished guides.

Trying to thank all those with whom I have shared a stream or river or lake over five-plus decades is next to impossible. I hope you all know how much you have meant to me.

There are a few very special and patient people who have taken time to read and comment on various parts of what follows as it grew, and whose honest critique, comments and input have been invaluable. My appreciation goes to Tim Landis, Patty Broyles, Norma Wechsler, John Endsley, Terry Allen, Bob Matthews, Bill and Annie Atchison, Byron and Paula Begley, Mike Alberti, Doyle Moore, Stan Welch, Quentin Cook and Carl Altizer for what they have contributed to this book.

But my final and most heartfelt thoughts and undying love and thanks are reserved for my dear wife Mary Jane and our daughter Carly and, of course, for Mom and Dad, who along with my sister and brothers, Beth, Alan and Jack, have always been here for me and who were there *with* me for much of what follows.

And now as I sit here alone at the end of this long dirt road looking back across so many years of fine water, fine fish and even finer companions, the red sun is setting across the dusky river in front of me.

And as I stand and look into its fading form, I think I see three figures beckoning me to cross.

Don't worry Little Hawk. I'll wait for you there.

X

· CONTENTS ·

XII

XIV

• FOREWORD •

This is a little embarrassing. When I asked my friend if he would write the foreword to this book, I didn't know what I was getting myself into.

To simply have him *like* the book would have been plenty for me, but his response set me back. After all, the man is a heck of a writer himself, and one of the finest and most generous people I have ever been privileged to know, not to mention a pretty fair fisherman.

Here was his response . . .

Hi Mike,

I've attached a draft of the foreword. I tried the standard format and failed. It just sounded like every other darn foreword out there and I hated it. Then I got the idea of doing it as an actual note to you.

If you don't dig it, let me know and I'll do a more standard one. Or, if you think I've missed the boat completely and want someone else to have a go at it, I'll certainly understand! No foul!

The book is GREAT and deserves an equally good foreword.

Flip

Hey Mike,

How do you do it? I'm a writer myself . . . it's all right to tell me. And you know I'll keep it to myself. How do you take a fishing day, and turn it into a fishing lifetime using the written word?

Sure, I'll write the foreword to your book, but you've got to give me a hint as to how a fella weaves family, fish, the sounds of a stream, the colors of fall and gifts from the Lord into a chronicle of *The Last Best Day*.

How is it that you are able to hear the thoughts of trout as they're being released? I have caught thousands of them and continue to listen to the silence of their beating gills as I remove every manner of fly from their upper jaws. Not a one has seen fit to utter a syllable in my direction.

Right now I'm leaning against a black mangrove, which pokes up through a rocky beach along the middle Florida Keys. I'm looking northwest and the sun will be gone within thirty minutes. A bonefish tail just shattered the surface of a shallow June evening. The manuscript of your book is in my right hand, where a fly rod should be. I want this foreword to be a good one Mike, up to the standards of what this book surely is.

I just wish you could see your way clear to divulge the process by which you're able to describe the photograph of a Dolly Varden and a bear track with such clarity! I'm actually seeing it . . . hell, I'm *smelling* it!

Folks reading *The Last Best Day* should understand that you didn't just sit down and write a book. I recognize *The Last Best Day* for what it is and know it to be – a chronicle of your outdoor lifetime – and as such, a chronicle of theirs and my own. It's your own personal search for not only the Giver, but for His Gift. If anyone's found it Mike, you have!

We all remember our first trout, turkey, elk, whitetail and yes, even the first smell of a skunk. I just wish you'd share the formula by which you are able to conjure up, or sometimes imagine, the minutia of those events. It's the glue that evaporates slowly with the passage of years for most of us. But not you. You're still able, after all the years, to navigate "the limitless abyss of a young man's imagination" and slip through the fog and pull right up to the dock. Your internal lodestone is an example to us all.

I expect that I'll just have to reread the book and divine the answers for myself. I further expect that's only as it should be as each of us crosses life's long or short fetch of water, pulling up to the dock that you've already tied to. Thanks Mike, for letting us peek at *"The Last Best Day"* and for the surety that the answers are "Out There."

Ever Your Friend,
Flip Pallot

• INTRODUCTION •

And so it is finally finished. For now, I have nothing more to write. At least nothing that I can write well and write to completion and be happy for the writing. It is all done, and I am empty and alone and quiet.

Perhaps someday on some page I might be able to connect the stranger who tried to get me to foul-hook the trout when I was eight years old, to the shameless snagging of the salmon I witnessed in Michigan when I was thirty-four. Perhaps someday I will finally be able to adequately organize the words and express the depth and feeling of that one sublime hour in my mid-fifties when I sat alone in the middle of a great Alaska river as it flowed timeless around me where one of its broad and moveable shoals had paused for a few brief decades to break the water's flow, and how that evening I actually became a part of the river.

Then I will tell you how the little gravel bar slowly formed below me as the great chinook salmon pulsed their way upriver, each on his or her own individual odyssey, their backs partly out of the water and so close that I could occasionally reach out and touch their royal scarlet shoulders as they made their way past me, surging upstream from the Bering Sea to find the places where they themselves had become Kings.

Then perhaps I will connect them with the other chinook at Harrisville on the western rim of Lake Huron, who were far too large to ever fit into the diminutive mouth of the little creek where they had been dumped as children before making their way downstream and out into the third Great Lake to grow into the great salmon they had now become, and how I waded out onto the bar to net a fish for the old man who had hooked one honestly as he stood among the snaggers on shore who made no real

XVIII

attempt to disguise their scavenging. Then I will tell you how hundreds of egg- and-sperm-laden salmon flowed around me there offshore as they circled at the mouth of the tiny creek, viewing me simply as one more obstacle to be avoided in their futile attempt to get back home.

Perhaps someday I will tell you what it was like to take my little sister fly fishing for the first time after a life of seeing her brothers and her dad leave for the streams, or about the wild angels my brothers and I ran into up on Frog Level, or maybe write the story about the snow monster who once haunted the south slopes of Holston Mountain.

But not now. Not tonight. I am all used up and spent. I have lived all the fishing I can live for now and written all I can tell well. So I will pause for a while and regroup and not fish again until the fishing itself calls of its own accord. For the time being I am peacefully, blissfully drained, neither hungering nor thirsting for the next adventure or the next stream, but instead waiting patiently for the desire to return in her own good time.

Only then will I once more feel compelled to gather my fly rods and my duffel and my cameras, and again slip my old bullet-and-bone pen and little lined journal into my pocket and hit the road or hit the sky and then hit the water and once more leave my boot prints in sand or gravel or mud as yet untrodden.

Michael Altizer
Watauga, Tennessee
July 14, 2007

I

If when I die, you'd plant a tree,

Not pluck the flower that feeds the bee

That gently sings inside of me,

Then I would live in forest tall,

My eyrie heights untouched by all

Save sparrow's nest and eagle's call.

THE LAST BEST DAY

"... if he could not fish and live
his life the way he wanted to,
he might as well be dead already.
He'd told them so."

He stood cold in the gathering dawn, peering deep into the chilled, flowing water. A sudden shiver ran through him, partly from the fresh winter wind and partly from the thrill he felt every time he came back to this secluded little stream. He had looked forward to this day for so long; indeed, the anticipation of returning here was the thing that had sustained him for months. He had no way of knowing that he was already halfway through his final year.

But now that I think about it, maybe he did.

Dying was no big deal. He'd already died once, and except for the efforts of some very committed people, he'd have gone on then. Now the memory of that day and the days that followed were like an aged and faded photograph to him, one slightly out of focus with the color mostly gone and the edges only a little less blurred than the center. Somehow it was an image too dim and unimportant for him to care about keeping. Today only the stream and the trout mattered. Dying was no big deal.

Since the heart attack, people who loved him had urged him to take things easier, or at least not to go fishing alone. He knew it was unrealistic to expect them all to understand that his best medicine would be the solitude he'd found here on this stream nearly a lifetime ago. But he also knew that if he couldn't fish and live his life the way he wanted to, he might as well be dead already. He'd told them so.

The little spring-fed creek flows into the uppermost lake where the big trout spend their summers feeding and fattening and waiting for the seasons to change to the time they can return to the places where they themselves became trout. Back in the early fifties, he'd had a hard time believing the rumors he'd heard about the big fish that were supposed to live here. But he and his cousin Verlin had finally found the little creek where the giant trout returned in winter.

Now it was *he* who returned, seeking his own continuity. Standing by the edge of the stream, he sensed for the first time since the heart attack that this life was once again truly his own and that he was finally free to carry his still-weakened heart down to the edge and into the cold, fuming water. It would be all right.

He walked back to the car and poured himself a cup of coffee from the old Thermos, sipping it slowly as he pulled on his waders. He'd always had a cigarette before as he did this, but now a cigarette was strictly out of the question. He felt grit beneath his toes when he stood, but he didn't want to spend the energy it would cost to pull the waders off and clear them.

Anyway, it really didn't matter; the sand was from this stream, and he knew there would likely be more.

He lifted his old fiberglass fly rod from behind the seat and eased the two sections together, rolling the cold metal ferrule against his oily forehead before slipping it into place. He had tied on a bare, freshly sharpened hook the night before and attached two tiny split-shot to the drop-line. Now he removed one of them, for the water was running a little low this morning.

He unscrewed the lid from one of his granddaughters' old baby food jars and lifted out an egg sack he had tied last winter. He carefully eased it past the barb and stuck the point of the hook into the scarred cork handle of the fly rod. Then, sliding the jar back into his vest pocket, he closed the car door without locking it and eased down the trail to the stream.

H is first few steps into the water were nearly a Baptism. It was good to sense the ancient gravel beneath his feet and once more feel the familiar details of the streambed telegraphed up the rod into his bare, warming hands as the split-shot rode the water-worn gravel where newly deposited trout lay awaiting their births. The winter wind was clear and sweet and it gently stung the tender lining of his clearing lungs as he recalled all the trout and all the men he had come to know on this creek, absent this morning of all human life but his own.

He worked the water smoothly and methodically, with an expertise and economy of effort that comes only with a lifetime of trout fishing. He had been casting for twenty minutes when his bare fingers began to chill, and he thought about moving on. But he made one more cast slightly upstream into the edge of the current and felt the line sweep along the bottom past him. Then as he lifted his rod at the end of the drift, he recognized an old familiar pressure.

He accelerated his lift and felt the full power of the trout as it erupted into the air, its silver sides kissed with crimson as it hung there broadside in a singular shaft of morning amber. Then, just as suddenly, the hook pulled from its gaping jaw and the trout twisted back into the water and was gone. It had won its battle, but so too had he. Already it had been a good day.

By 11:30 he had worked his way up past the bridge, nearly all the way to the little white church that sits on a small hill overlooking the stream, and he found himself quietly singing along with some of the more familiar songs as they drifted across the meadow toward him. Finally, he returned to the car and drove down to the falls; but he knew it would be unwise to descend the trail here, for he would eventually have to climb back out.

Still, as he surveyed this magnificent stretch of water, he unconsciously dissected each run below him with his memory and could almost *feel* the streambed as his steel-blue eyes danced across the moving surface of the water, and he thought about some of the trout he'd taken here.

There below Cook Hollow was the six-and-a-half pounder that had led him on such a wild run before Verlin had finally been able to net it. And here below the falls was the twenty-four inch rainbow his young son had fished over for nearly thirty minutes. The boy had eventually grown impatient and moved, only to see his Dad hook the trout on his third drift. It had taken nearly fifteen minutes to land the fish, and a crowd of other fishermen had gathered to watch as he finally brought it to net.

He remembered how proud his boy had been as together they'd carried the great fish up the steep slope to the car. Back then they often kept the trout they caught, for these were men who frequently fed their families from the providence of their streams. Many times he and his boy had lain face down together on the hanging rock at the head of the falls and watched as the fish leapt their way upstream to find the ancient gravel beds where they themselves had been spawned.

But on this cold, perfect morning, he had no way of seeing his son down there alone in the warm pre-dawn light six months from now, fishing a few small stones from the stream to bring back and place beside him in his casket.

Suddenly he realized he was hungry – not simply ready for some lunch, but really *hungry*. It was good to be hungry again. He walked back to the car and unwrapped one of the sandwiches his wife had made for him the night before. The flavors of the cold meats had mingled delicately with the homemade bread and the rich brown mustard, and the hot coffee felt soothing as it followed the sandwich down.

He felt so good. This was the best day he'd had in months. It was nice to feel good again; he'd had such a good morning; perhaps now was a good time to leave.

But *no*. He was enjoying himself too much to leave. He knew where he could fish, not far upstream at a place where he wouldn't have to climb so far down to the creek. In ten minutes he was there.

He parked next to the old stone barn and cinched up his hip-waders. Then with his fly rod in hand, he crossed the barbed wire fence where the top strand went missing twenty years ago and started walking toward the sound of living water.

I wish I knew how it happened. I wish I knew every delicious detail of how he caught that trout. He called me that night to tell me about it, but I was too excited to get all the details, and he was too excited to tell. Now I don't remember whether he caught it on an egg sack or on one of the little yarn patterns he'd learned to tie in Michigan. I don't know whether he hooked it above the riffle that splits the run or below it.

I don't even know what color shirt he wore.

But I *do* know he kept that trout above him. He would always try to apply downstream pressure to a big fish as soon as he hooked it and then rely on its instinct to resist the pull and head upstream. It's much easier to play a fish if you can stay below it where it can't use the force of the current against you. He taught me this when I was a little boy.

I know he played that trout as carefully as any fish he ever caught, for though he had his old net strung across his right shoulder, he didn't use it. I know the fish weighed about three-and-a-half pounds, because he said so. I know it was a female, swollen with still-forming trout.

And I know that when he finally worked her in close to the edge, Dad knelt down in the cold water, carefully slipped the hook from the corner of her mouth, and watched his last Rainbow slowly swim away.

CHAPTER 1

THE GIVERS

"God didn't have to create trout;
He could have settled for bass."

"Behold, I will send for many fishers,
saith the Lord, and they shall fish . . . "
– Jeremiah 16:16

God didn't have to create trout; He could have settled for bass.

Please don't misunderstand me; I have nothing against bass. Properly perceived and properly done, fishing of any sort is a gentle reflection of life itself in all its ungentle realities, where we as fishermen encounter that which we know and love as well as that which we simply endure, and sometimes even that which is repulsive. I enjoy bass fishing from time to time, but bass are not an integral part of where I come from or who I am, and they are certainly not something I absolutely *need*. Not the way I need trout.

But as I think about it, neither did God need trout, any more than He needed walnuts or amethyst or ibis or me. Personally, I think He just *wanted* them, and it seems now that trout have become one of His great equalizers, for anyone who catches even the most diminutive trout, whether with spun glass or woven graphite or finely crafted bamboo or even common cut cane cannot help but be uplifted by the encounter, regardless of rank or wealth. For the blessing lies in the trout and not the tackle.

When I consider just how much of my life has been spent without trout, either on the far end of a fly line or in the stream of life that flows around me, I realize that each moment I spend in their company is truly a gift from their Creator, and it is this reality that constantly reminds me that God Himself is *Creative*.

But what does it mean to be Creative? What does it mean to create? What is its purpose, and more importantly, what is its hope? I have often tried to imagine what God might have been thinking in the pre-Big Bang phase of the universe He was then only contemplating:

"We will need Light. And space.

And water; we'll definitely need water. And carbon and oxygen; that's it! We'll base it all on a carbon-oxygen exchange.

Now let's see, what else?

We'll need gravity and inertia. And the creatures will likely fare better if they have some familiar and accessible frame of reference by which to measure their living.

What can we do about that . . . let's see; how about Time.

We will need plankton and poetry and ice. And the air and water will need to be constantly redistributed, so it should be a closed system more or less, where everything is used and reused.

Okay, that should do for a Beginning.

Now . . . Let There Be Light."

When He finally spoke, the *Bang* must indeed have been *Big*, as all subsequent evidence has clearly indicated. And so as His creative processes continued to evolve, I imagine He saw it was going quite well, thank you. So He continued to conceptualize and build, learning as He patiently progressed, working on the whole and constantly refining the details.

It seems perfectly clear that He provided everything that was absolutely necessary, but He also seems to have created some things simply for the sheer, unfettered joy of creation: Bananas, Sunsets, Bird Songs, Orion.

Autumn. Saturn. Woodgrain. *Trout.*

Trout! How did God ever come up with the idea for Trout?

Surely it must have been a moment of divine inspiration, for there were to be such interesting and sublime variations on the theme: Rainbows and Cutthroats, Browns, Goldens, Ohrids, each so different yet each so alike, so masterfully gifted that there could be no doubt as to the Giver.

It was clear from the beginning that God would deal only in originals.

And then there were Brook Trout. Can you imagine His glee when He came up with the idea for Brook Trout? I wonder if God giggles. I wonder if for a moment He thought this might be just a little too much.

Well, maybe not. After all, He'd already done the Auroras and Arroyos and Luna Moths and the Morning Star and had hidden the mysteries of ice for us to discover someday for ourselves. Take a break. Read Genesis.

This was special.

But now, what to make of it; what to actually *do* with trout? Surely he realized that these creatures were much too distinctive to be a mere link in the food chain, though that would have to do for a start.

But could trout perhaps eventually be an end in themselves? No, that would constrain them. *Could they then be an occasional occurrence, rarely seen, like a comet or a mantis, therefore precious in their rarity?* No, that would limit the potential of the gift. And then, perhaps, it hit Him:

This is their real value . . . as a *Gift.*

And so the Giver bestowed the Gift, scattered jewels in streams of gold, succulent to the palate and gratifying to the senses of those destined to be blessed with their very own trout. For it is clear that He already had the concept of angling in mind and has since been known to keep close company with fishermen. Still, the thought of man catching wholesale quantities of trout in great nets must have dissuaded Him and caused Him to consider other, more subtle methods of bringing humans and trout together. So now He must have pondered technique.

I wonder if He came up with the food structure first, or the idea of the fly. He had to make certain there would be insects and crustaceans and other fish and even small mammals that man could eventually imitate with the materials at hand. For if man were indeed to be made in God's own image, then man must be creative as well.

And finally, how best to present these offerings? His experiments had probably already confirmed what He'd suspected from the beginning: that materials and spirits that bend are stronger and more resilient than those that do not. So a little refinement here and a minor adjustment there, all combined with the measured application of divine anticipation and thought, and finally the concept: *Bamboo*.

Thus Trout became a Gift, serving the spirit of man and the Spirit of God alike. For it still seems to be supremely gratifying to Him each time a trout takes a fly, whether it is one cast by Him, or by you, or by me.

And He places His gifts in such lovely places, not only in the physical world, but also in those deeper recesses of our souls. Now when I fish, the scope of why I am here is ever broadened. It isn't simply for the trout; they are merely the vehicles that first brought me to the water and continue to bring me back. But to what end?

There can *be* no end. For if I were ever to finalize this process of fishing, or for that matter of life itself, there would be no more anticipation, no more growth, no more sweet vacancy in my soul waiting to be filled. Should I ever perfect my technique, my understanding, my sense of why I am here, I would no longer feel compelled to seek that which I cannot comprehend, to touch what I cannot hold, and to know Him who created both the trout and me. I might even mistake myself as being complete, and therefore fail to understand that I must continually strive to be *His* brush rather than my *own* painting. For the Gift is always of greatest value to the *Giver*.

B ut if it was God who gave me the gift of trout, it was Dad who gave me the gift of trout *fishing*. And later, so much later, there was yet another who repaired and restored the Gift and so helped it grow from the tattered remnants of something far too painful to contemplate retrieving on my own.

Chapter 2

Surface Tension

_____

_____

"For a moment I glimpsed the Eternal,
if only as a trout who once in a mighty leap
to free himself might have glimpsed the world
that exists above the surface tension."

do not want to write this story. I should not have to write this story. The fact is, I'm not certain I could, even if I wanted to, for it is not my story to write. I told my brother he would probably have to write it himself, for he could see it far more clearly than I.

I could only fear.

How would it be to go back? I had not set foot in that stream since the morning years earlier when I'd fished a few small stones from its gravel bed to take back and place beside our Dad as he lay still in his casket.

Well, perhaps *fear* isn't the right word.

It's just that Dad's life had been so entwined with this stream, the stream's life so much a part of our own. We'd first fished it together, Dad and I, when he was young and I was new, and now that I think about it, I had never fished it without him. My brother wasn't even sure where it was exactly, and I had to give him directions and tell him where he could park and how to find the trail that leads down to the falls.

And he caught trout. Fresh, pink, skillet trout. Trout that our mother had craved for too many years without telling any of us. Trout that no one else had been able to catch for her in a very long time and that she fried up fresh for the two of them that very night.

e just wouldn't give it up, my little brother. And he was so slick. He did not push and cajole; he simply fished and left it up to Mom to tell me how good it was. She always did like him best, and he didn't do anything to make it better for me. He says to this day that Mom and Dad kept having kids until they finally got one right, while I have always held the position that they did such a fine job on the eldest that they kept trying, without success, to match the result. This has been an ongoing point of discussion between my brother Jack and me for years, but I have always secretly known that *he* is the one who is right.

So . . . would I like to hit Doe Creek? Well, uh, sure. I guess.

I showed him the special places and told him their names and some of the stream's fabled history. I took him to the Old Mill Hole where Mr. Wilson had taken the twelve-pound, ten-ounce state record rainbow that stood for decades. I showed him Cook Hollow and the Sarge Hole and told him about the Jake Hole, but I couldn't recall where it was.

I really should know where the Jake Hole is, but I can't remember. I guess I'll have to ask Verlin. Verlin will remember.

took him to the Bridge Hole and the Telephone Pole Hole, and he showed me a run he'd been calling "The Stump" and asked me if we'd ever caught trout there. *Are these names too much?* I really don't care; that's what they were, and now I may be the only one who remembers them, for none of the old Doe Creek fishermen took their sons very often.

Except, of course, for Dad.

Now, the creek is populated with run-of-the-mill stockers and is just one more name in the state fishing regulations, and hardly anyone seems to know or much care that its native strain of giant, lake-run rainbows once held tremendous promise.

Finally we descended to the falls, just like Dad and I used to do. It was strange to be warm here, for Doe Creek had always been a winter place with the great trout up from Watauga Lake to spawn, small in number but large in girth. Now it was June, and the trout my brother had been catching here were hatchery fish with one fin clipped and not much color. I couldn't help but wonder if any of the old strain had survived the misbegotten efforts of the state to manage their existence by constructing a few rock dams that were too high and the road that now paralleled the creek.

Jack was already in the water when I reached the bottom of the trail, and he showed me where he had just seen a trout roll. I fished it through as best I could from where I stood, but I only got hung up and had to break the line.

But no matter; I needed to change the tippet anyhow, and the blood knot seemed to tie itself as I watched my Dad . . . *excuse me* . . . my brother, fish. And as for the rest of the day, well as I said, that is Jack's story to write.

B ut it wasn't about the past. It really wasn't even about Dad. It was about the moment at hand, about my brother and me finally catching up with ourselves and moving forward, just as Dad had tried to tell us all along we would.

Is what he gave us any less tangible just because he died? I don't think so. If anything it is stronger and more resilient; there is nothing else he could do for us that has not already been done, but there is still plenty for *us* to do with those who have meaning in our lives. In the end, that's all they'll have left of us anyway.

For a moment I glimpsed the Eternal, if only as a trout who once in a mighty leap to free himself might have glimpsed the world that exists above the surface tension. He cannot begin to comprehend it, but at least he has seen it.

Next time, I'll fish.

– Chapter 3 –

Between Brothers

"Sometimes we are fly fishermen
and sometimes we are trout fishermen.
Sometimes we are both."

There are things between brothers that bind and things between brothers that cleave. And it really doesn't much matter which, for they cannot be forgotten, nor oftentimes should they be. Some are timeless and soothing, and some are stressful and hurt like briars. Still, if the brothers are sensible and care about one another, these things between them, whether painful or sublime, are nurtured and become causes for growth and celebration and strengthened bonds.

There has never been any pain between my brother Jack and me. For us, fishing has always been a good thing. Sometimes we are fly fishermen and sometimes we are trout fishermen. Sometimes we are both.

When we are fly fishermen, I dearly love to send a March Brown or a Royal Wulff along the edge of a clear mountain run and imagine what may see it as it dances down the current. Sometimes I even hope the trout will leave the fly alone because it stands so nicely on the water.

My brother, on the other hand, is partial to larger waters and usually fishes a beadhead Prince Nymph or a weighted Stonefly or Wooly Bugger deep along the bottom where the big trout feed. His offerings often yield more and larger trout than mine. But certainly no more satisfaction.

But when we are trout fishermen, we are by definition out for trout, and no perfect tight loop or drag-free drift is allowed to come between us and our purpose. Otherwise, we might as well be reading books instead of water, for nothing short of actually feeling the trout will do. At such times, perhaps a dry fly is indeed the best thing to have at the end of a tippet; but if chunk-and-dunk is required, then chunk-and-dunk it shall be, and woe to the elitist who would stand in our way. Especially the elitist within.

We will gladly sacrifice form for this purist of pleasures. And whether at the end of the catching we ease the trout back into the water or into the creel for our supper, it does not diminish the primordial sense of conquest we gain in overcoming none but ourselves. For it is not the trout we have bettered, nor even each other.

I am as pleased with my brother's victories as he is with mine. I do not have to be better than him or even better than the trout; I simply have to be better than the person I was just a few moments earlier.

D ad would have gotten such a kick out of these last few days, seeing Jack and me exploring new water together on the creek we've found, just as he and Verlin had done on Doe Creek nearly fifty years ago.

I won't tell you the name of the new creek; you wouldn't believe it anyway if you knew where it was. But when I netted Jack's twenty-one-inch rainbow, when I held up my own nineteen-inch prize for him to see, when he yelled for me to come help him net another three-and-a-half-pounder even though he knew I was far upstream and he could easily have netted it himself . . . it was Dad and Verlin all over again.

No competition. Neither of us trying to better the other. It wasn't about image or technique or who had the best equipment. It was simply the unfettered joy of fishing together and not having to explain or apologize to anyone, especially ourselves, for the pure pleasure of simply sharing such a wonderful time.

Just Jack, hoping I would catch a trout this morning because he had caught one yesterday evening, and me, hoping he would catch a trout this afternoon because I had caught one this morning. And now both of us, 120 miles apart, wishing we hadn't lost that hook-jawed thrasher this evening at dusk in the rain-swollen bend below the Crease.

But I have four meetings in three cities next week, and Jack's leave from the military is nearly over, and it's almost time for him to disappear from the world yet again as he heads back to wherever his well-worn green beret may dictate until he resurfaces and wants to go for trout once more.

So for now I would much rather look back to the last couple of days than forward to the next.

We weren't entirely certain whether we actually saw the three trout yesterday morning before the rains came or just their shadows against the rocky streambed. But there they were all the same, one giant and two followers. We judged them to be one large female with a dominant male and a smaller satellite rainbow tagging along, hoping to get lucky.

They cruised up and down the Bridge Pool, alternately disappearing into the deep, root-bound head of the run and then reappearing twenty yards downstream. We could not get a response from any of them, so while I worked another trout holding in front of a large rock at the tail of the pool, Jack concentrated on a dark undulating shadow deep along the edge of the current just above the footbridge.

Neither of us could generate any interest at all from the fish, and I finally moved up to see what my brother was doing. He had tried most everything in his fly box without success, so when I offered him my five-weight with a black Wooly Bugger, he took it without hesitation.

We both saw the trout's bright side flash as he rolled on the fly, and I ditched Jack's rod and dashed in below him with my net as he barked orders. He knew precisely where he needed me to be, and I was altogether confident in his directions. I moved slightly downstream to clear the water for them both, keeping the trout between us, and then watched as my brother played it to perfection, so that in the end all I had to do was lift the net at the right moment and hand it to him.

The trout's colors were vivid and deep, and we could tell she had been upstream from the lake for a while. I pulled the camera from my coat pocket and recorded Jack gently reviving the fish and easing her back into her world. Then with great exclamations and a good high-five, we relived the moments just passed.

And though darkness overtook us before we could locate another trout, we knew exactly where we would be come daylight.

20

cy rain greeted us at midnight. And when we got back to the stream this morning the trees were sheathed in a thin veneer of rime, and the cold mist was turning to a steady drizzle. We had promised ourselves and our mother that if either of us caught a big male today, we would have trout for supper. But as we eased down the trail and neared the first bend, we marked the richened color of the creek and its rising water and knew that our prospects for dinner looked dim.

We saw no sign of yesterday afternoon's trio at the Bridge Pool, and after a few pointless drifts we continued downstream, sight-fishing from the trail as we moved. I finally dropped off to check a good-looking run eighty yards below the footbridge while Jack moved in fifty yards below me.

I can't quite figure out what drew me to that little run; there were other, better looking options both upstream and down, and I should have been able to detect a trout if it was there, even in the cloudy water. But still I made one good cast into the head of the current, just out of curiosity.

The hit didn't even feel like a hit; something just felt different. But I learned long ago to pay particular attention to differences, like seeing an emptiness in a tangled thicket in rain that turns out to be a deer, or a slight uneven ripple along the river's edge that becomes a wood duck.

It was just something out of place, not as it should be, and I struck.

y the time I saw the trout, he was rolling away from me as my line and fly cleared the water, connected only to the air. Jack didn't see him, but he certainly heard my exclamation as I verbally expressed disappointment in how poorly I had fished. I made one more cast out of sheer frustration, but I knew my best bet would be to rest the fish for a while.

I moved on downstream, leapfrogging Jack and checking the water below the falls. I watched as he fished down to the bend above me, both our minds still upstream. We've caught trout before that have been hooked just fifteen or twenty minutes earlier; some say to wait, but I think that if a fish is in a feeding mode, you are often better served taking advantage of it, especially if the trout has not been hooked hard.

I backed out and let Jack fish through, watching him work the water to perfection. For my part, I waited the requisite twenty minutes and then headed back upstream. I whistled for Jack a couple of times, but he was now far below and could not hear me.

Alone once more, I approached the trout I'd moved a few minutes earlier, easing up the trail above him and then coming in from the same direction I had come in before, figuring if he hadn't seen me then, he shouldn't see me now. Once in position, I cast upstream, well above where I had last seen him, and frankly I don't remember now whether it was the first drift or the second he took. But I do remember how it felt – a short, quick, pulsing hesitation, and again I struck.

I was below the trout when he hit, and he bolted upstream, away from the pressure of the rod. I cannot say how long he was on, but he rolled and thrashed and tried to throw whatever it was that held him. And just as I had the net in position beneath him, the line went sickeningly slack and I lifted my net straight up, not at all certain whether or not the trout was actually in it.

When next I spotted my brother he was fully absorbed in getting his line out of an overhanging tree limb and just happened to look up and see me standing there in the trail.

"Tryin' for squirrels?" I called.

He scowled and growled and made some threatening gestures and then continued rummaging for his fly. When he finally looked back, I held the big trout aloft for him to see and he completely forgot about his tangled line. You know, the boy really shouldn't try to dance like that in a swollen stream, especially with his eyes so wide open.

Our supper now secure, we moved back up toward the bridge, and as we approached the run, Jack whispered, *"Big trout!"*

You can tell it's a really big trout when someone as normally unexcitable as my brother *whispers* an exclamation point. I took up position at the tail of the run, and of course the trout moved upstream to Jack. Oh well, it was his turn anyhow, so I worked above him and was a good eighty yards away when I heard him yell.

I knew the routine by now and again I ditched my fly rod in a convenient stand of reeds and sprinted over hill, over dale, oversized net in hand. I slipped in below Jack and netted the trout within a few feet of where I had netted the first one yesterday evening. Same routine, same exclamations, same high five . . . how about that, you *can* dance in a rain-swollen stream.

It was another male, about twenty inches, so we decided to keep him for Mom to have later, and we continued fishing upstream. Jack explained how the first to catch a fish on days ending with the letter "Y" is responsible for carrying all the fish kept that day. It's some sort of law or principle or creed or something. At my advanced age, I still can't figure out how I've missed that one all these years. I guess he picked it up out West or perhaps in his Special Forces training. Then again, maybe I'm just getting easy.

At any rate, we continued upstream where I located a trout just below the first bend. But I could not get him to respond.

When we got up to the Crease, Jack spotted one holding hard against the undercut bank on his side of the creek. As he worked that fish, I located another holding downstream in a strong back-eddy, but neither of us could coax a hit. My trout finally moved out of his lie when I showed him a bright pink egg pattern. From this and the same result I'd gotten with a salmon streamer yesterday evening, we determined that these are manly trout who simply do not go for pink.

While I was engrossed in my color research, Jack also lost sight of his fish for a moment, and when they reappeared, both trout were together down at the tail end of the pool. We were on opposite sides of the creek by now, Jack to my left as we faced upstream, and we alternated our offerings to the two big rainbows.

We tried varying presentations, but when I quartered mine cross-current right over the largest trout's head, it swirled from its lie, and with mouth gaping wide and white, it inhaled the fly and then twisted back toward the tail of the chute. We each clearly saw the take, and as I struck, both the trout and my brother bolted downstream into the next run.

I was able to keep the fish there for a moment, just long enough for Jack to get into position below it. We were well into the bend of the creek now, and I held my place, for the trout had moved slightly back up toward me in response to Jack's movements below. For the moment I concentrated on simply maintaining consistent pressure on the fish, for it was obvious that we were going to be here for a while.

The rainbow held deep for the next minute or so, though I could feel him shaking his head occasionally. I moved a few yards downstream to decrease the angle on him, and in response he began working the strong current.

He first moved slightly upstream, then made a quick dash down toward Jack and swirled again at the tail of the run. Moving downstream himself, Jack worked into position below us, hoping the trout would drift backward toward him.

The strategy was good, but my brother's first attempt only got half the trout into the net; that's all the net he had. The fish kicked out and moved into the edge of the fast-moving run between us, now holding hard up against the rocks, and once again Jack got all the net he had around all the fish he could. But once more the trout kicked free, this time bolting downstream. Big time! And just as I was finalizing my decision as to what to get my brother for Christmas, he yelled, "I'm going to need *your* net!"

24

The trout was now holding firm in the short chute below us. As I reached for the net, I transferred the line from my left hand to my right, pressing it firmly and securely against the cork handle of the rod.

And now I flash back to this morning's trout and the line gone slack as I slipped the net beneath him. But this time the net is still on my shoulder, and my brother's pained expression mirrors my own as we both see the light fly line suddenly hanging limp, suspended and disconnected in the air between us before settling impotently back down onto the surface of the stream, and the trout's broad crimson side flashing free and deep in the pool below us as he disappears.

There was nothing to do except endure the sudden emptiness and realize what we should have done just a few seconds ago. But Eternity itself is now closer than *"just a few seconds ago,"* for Eternity shall indeed come. But the past, though hanging limp in the air around us like my fly line seconds earlier, is gone forever.

Still, just losing that trout was more fulfilling than most things I've ever actually accomplished.

And now the rain finally began to penetrate my wools, and for the first time I noticed the slow chill beginning to creep into my arms and shoulders. My brother's high-tech jacket had kept him perfectly cozy, and when we climbed back out to the truck, I stripped off my wet sweater and shirt. As I replaced them with something dry, Jack pulled his own warm stocking cap down over my head, murmuring something about hypothermic principles and heat-loss.

He started up my truck with his spare key as I fished out some oatmeal cakes, and since he was already behind the wheel, I slid into the shotgun seat and sat back to enjoy the ride up and out and back into the world, where it is now raining again as we approach midnight.

It feels as though it may turn to snow.

have a breakfast meeting in the morning at 7:15 in Knoxville and then fly out for St. Louis at 1:20. By then Jack will be back with his unit on a C-*something-or-other* on his way to a place I promise you I would not want to be going.

But if I told you where, he'd have to do away with us both.

CHAPTER 4

TO KILL A TROUT

" . . . a trout is a gift,
and so must on occasion be received,
whole and alive, to be savored
to the last morsel . . . "

ishing for trout is about far more than simply *catching* trout, and anyone who cannot fathom this fact had best stick to bass. A trout is spirit and contemplation and therefore should neither be approached nor accepted without a considerable degree of reverence and appreciation.

A trout should never be perceived as a *trophy*, and he who would dare presume to "harvest" a wild trout should consider taking down his fly rod and using it for agriculture instead of encounter, for he is quite likely incapable of more.

This is not to say that a trout should never be killed, for he who does not know the taste and texture of his very own trout is still little more than a tourist who has not yet ventured off the beaten trail in an effort to explore and experience the full measure of his sojourn, his cup filled, overflowing its confining brim, spilling forth its contents in an overwhelming baptism of association and truth.

The fisherman who would not on occasion partake of his own trout has not yet realized the full measure of the Gift.

o properly catch a trout, one must first care about trout and think of them individually, as something more than a mere trophy, whether that trophy is intended to occupy a wall or a memory. *Never* keep score with trout. Trout are not units of measure to be numbered and tallied and recorded in self-serving downstream conversation, either with others or with oneself.

Instead, each trout should be savored as you savor a thought, slowly and deliberately turning it over in your experience and exploring its meaning as you explore the deep, delicate colors and intricate patterns that grace its elegant sides. These individual markings are God's own signature, bearing witness to the fact that He has personally touched this creature and validated it for encounter by anyone who might care enough to experience it.

For though His gifts are plentiful, they should neither be accepted lightly nor viewed without the proper appreciation of their meaning and of the thought, effort and cost that has gone into their creation.

And so it was that yesterday I killed a trout.

I hooked her up in the Otter Pool, below the bedrock ledge that diagonals downstream before disappearing beneath the mountain. She took a small Sparrow Wing my brother Alan had tied and headed off in the general direction of *away* before I could even begin to think about commencing negotiations with her.

Her furious cross-stream momentum quickly had me playing catch-up as I followed her out across the rocky streambed. I was relieved when she finally surfaced for a quick look around before all the line had cleared my antique brass Sunnybrook fly reel. But if I had any thought or hope that things were going to get easier from this point, I was badly mistaken.

She was evidently not at all satisfied with her position and so reversed course and headed back upstream to where she had begun her run, passing close enough to me that I could have swatted her with my little three-weight if I hadn't been so busy stripping line in a desperate attempt to keep some semblance of a direct connection with her.

Now she was back on her own turf, and we both had some hard decisions to make: should she jump in an attempt to rid herself of this thing that held her, or should she burrow deep and try once more to flee?

For my part, I was concerned with the abuse my light tippet had just taken on its convoluted tour. For I knew her run had taken her across at least two submerged rock outcroppings, in addition to a large sunken snag that had been washed downriver in last spring's floods, and I hoped that my fluorocarbon leader was still up to the task.

It was now impossible to force the issue and turn her quickly, and I knew I would have to play her slowly and deliberately if I were to have any chance of bringing her to hand. But I also knew that she would likely be pretty well exhausted if I did manage to get her to the net, and for one brief moment I actually considered just pointing the rod tip at her and breaking her off right then and there.

But the fight thus far had already cost her dearly, and I could tell from the messages she was sending back up the line that she was nearly spent. And so when she finally turned in my direction and I could see her deep pink gill-plates and the broad crimson slash along her upturned side, I gently guided her head-first into the net and knew immediately she was coming home to dinner.

She measured just under twenty inches, and when I showed her to Eric last night when he stopped by to return a reel he had borrowed, he was quietly but obviously indignant.

I truly believe that Eric thinks trout fishing is a sport.

I fear that trout have become more of a disposable commodity for him than a spiritual experience, for he disposes of so many, releasing every trout he catches, regardless of its condition.

He would no more be caught keeping a trout than he would be seen fishing with monofilament.

It's simply not done.

Personally, I like having a meal or two of trout in the freezer, and I will never release a trout that I don't believe will survive; I have seen too many sportsmen spend far too much time handling or photographing a trout, then chunk their catch back into the water and look around and smile about what a conscientious sport they are.

Now as I sit here on this rock changing flies and peering into the water around me, I realize that I have never once seen a naturally dead trout, except of course in the clutches of an osprey or an eagle. And as I scan the marled streambed beneath my feet, I think I see why, for they always disappear so quickly once they leave my hand.

But I have seen them when they've been killed by a poorly timed or poorly executed release, even before they have actually succumbed to their injuries and died, erratically quivering sideways down the dark current or lying on their sides, bright and cold and sickly white against the bottom of the stream.

And most likely so have you.

I wonder what happens to old trout when their work here is done? Do they abandon their lifelong pursuit of the surface flies they once loved, now too weak to rise through the current to take them?

Do they become evermore weary and unable to dart sideways through the swifter waters to snap up a quick little minnow or a lightly rising nymph. Do they seek calmer waters, where the oxygen levels are diminished along with the speed of the flow?

Do they die as rapidly in the stream as they do with the eagle? Or do they linger for a time, seeking one more morsel to sustain them for just a moment longer before they go?

And what happens to them when finally they die?

Are they transformed into gold, ever coursing the streams of the Eternal, waiting patiently for something delicious they no longer require, waiting there for a sunset that never comes?

Waiting there for you and me?

I will have to admit that Eric is right about one thing: I could always buy a trout from the market. But he knows and I know that I never will. Any more than I will order one from a menu.

I simply can't bring myself to do it.

A true trout can never be bought; not with money or graphite or a vest full of equipment.

Remember, a trout is a Gift and so must on occasion be accepted whole and alive and savored to the last morsel.

He who does not from time to time know the taste of his very own trout is consigned to the empty fellowship of his elite brethren, starving for want of the basics and daring not to break the mold and partake of the sustenance that has been so graciously proffered.

Chapter 5

Quick Brown Fox

" . . . never had any morsel bitten back
at her with such vengeance . . . "

*S*he seethed like a trapped wolf, constrained by the cold hard steel that held her. But she still could move, and she moved quite well, thank you, now leaping as she had first leapt when she'd felt the hook bite into the white leathery tissue in the roof of her tooth-strewn mouth. But for the most part she simply sulked deep in the pool where earlier she had paused for a few hours to rest and feed during her relentless cruising up and down the river.

She had, in fact, been in this same pool since just before daybreak, having tarried here after the water had begun to go down as the generators in the dam upstream shut off on schedule at 5 A.M.

But that was another *creature's method of keeping time. For her, time was meaningless, life instead measured by cycles of day and night, darkness and light, smell and sight, as it had been for as long as she'd been a part of the river. Whether she had any concept of future or past, I cannot know. It really doesn't matter, for she had always lived in the present, occasionally sipping a fly from the surface, but now more often sifting the deeper currents for nymphs and probing the moss beds for scuds and sowbugs, and lately taking other fish and even her own kind for meals that had made her large in girth and quick in her reaction. But never had any morsel bitten back at her with such vengeance as had this little yellow-bodied, brown-winged delicacy now stuck in her jaw, which constrained her and confused her and caused her to grow more and more resentful with each passing moment.*

And she expressed herself so well, leaving no question as to her feelings or intent. Her powerful body undulated deep along the underside of the current, and her broad, flat, arrow-shaped head pierced the flow and was occasionally given to violent wrenching in a vain attempt to rid itself of this sinister sting that worked itself deeper with her every surge. The colors along her powerful sides rightly rippled through deepened shades of maple and purple and gold, an iridescent field of tone over which black dapples danced and butter-rimmed crimson orbs glowed like Chinese lanterns.

Yet strength was not the answer. She'd already tried being strong on her initial run upstream after her first panicked leap, and she leapt again in fear and frustration when she realized she couldn't outdistance this thing that held her. She had always been able to flee from danger and toward life, her quickness and stealth the only difference between eating or being eaten. From her perspective, it had been this way forever, always about the getting of meals, and it had never occurred to her that it could ever change.

But now she sensed a subtle shift, if a brown trout can ever sense subtlety, as her frustration grew into determination, and her fear turned into cold, controlled rage.

I remember that trout. From the moment I first heard her, I intended to have her. I listened as she fed from the thin, late-evening hatch that had barely materialized just before dusk. It took three long minutes in the waning light to tie a new piece of 6X tippet into my leader, my eyes long since hazed by the sun and wind.

It was sheer dumb luck that I happened to be watching the same caddis she was watching as it drifted into her sight window, for her take was barely perceptible in the warm evening light that brushed the frayed edges of the current she was working.

The sound she made as she fed was not a mere reckless surface splash, but instead a cool, liquid thump that resonated above the keen whisper of the river as it shredded itself on the rocks below.

Other trout and other fishermen were rising and cavorting and chasing anything that moved. But not her.

She jealously held her lie as though she had a significant allocation of life invested in its finding, and her measured, metered gulps bore stark evidence that her investment was paying handsome dividends.

I carefully circled to get into position below her, covering the last fifty feet or so as quietly as I could, and finally got within comfortable casting distance of where she was working. My little #18 CDC Comparadun was so perfect that a natural landed on it and rode it clear to the end of the drift. On my second cast she took another natural that floated just inches from my own bogus offering. It was obvious she wasn't buying what I was selling, so there was nothing to do but change the fly.

The minutes seemed to ooze as I fumbled in the fading light, listening to her methodical feeding as I focused on selecting a new pattern. It was clear that subtle deception was not the answer, so with time and daylight drifting downstream with the river, I opted for a #14 yellow-bodied Stimulator.

An errant wisp of wind caught my first cast, and the new fly landed short and slightly behind her. I let it drift far down-current before lifting it as gently as possible from the water, fervently hoping that a smaller trout would not take the fly. The second cast went long by a couple of feet, and I winced as the gossamer tippet passed mere inches above her. The third cast landed much too close to her, and I desperately tried to calm myself by pretending this was just a fish. But the pale yellow blur that swirled on my fly put an end to any thought of calm.

The big browns of the Clinch rarely leap, so when she cleared the water as I set the hook, it elevated my soul. But not hers. A brown trout has no soul. Souls are reserved for the fisherman and his kind, along with the accountability that most assuredly accompanies a soul.

But this trout did have *spirit*, as all trout do, and I was surprised when she took my fly three feet into the air as I struck. She did not hang for the requisite cliché moment in the low golden shaft of sunlight she penetrated, but instead twisted back into the edge of the current and burrowed deep, as though she had surprised even herself with the leap.

I knew immediately that she was a brown, for she was barely twenty feet in front of me and nearly at eye level at the top of her antic, and the low evening sunlight bore no evidence of coral along her buttery sides. But even had I not seen her, I would have known she was a brown trout, for her spirit betrayed her identity as she complained deep along the base of the current.

Did I mention she had spirit?

N ow no longer would she leap. Instead, she would focus her instincts on freeing herself from that which caused her to fear. No longer would she flee straight away; instead, her counterpoint movements indicated that she had consolidated her tactics and from here on would contend with her savvy as well as with her strength.

Out into the main flow she moved, still upstream, ever widening the gap between herself and fear. For the first time in the struggle, she felt a certain invigorating sense of control, which told her that indeed all was not lost and that she was still free to hope.

She continued cruising left, heading away into the current, and as she moved she sensed the constraining force moving with her until they were both once again nearly vertical to the flow. Again she gave her head a mighty shake, and in her anger she nearly leapt again. But with unplumbed self-discipline she constrained herself and settled back into the current. She could now feel strength flowing through her and out with the passing of the river, and she began to sense the need to make something happen to force this issue which she still couldn't understand.

I could feel her indignity as she sulked there upstream, and the smooth, controlled undulations of her sleek and sensual body indicated she had not yet decided what to do with me. So I simply let her think, applying only enough pressure to keep her honest. I didn't want to start playing her from the base of the little rod just yet; the tippet was not that strong, and I feared enlarging the tiny hole the hook had made in her mouth.

For a while she seemed content to stay more or less where she was ... or did she just reposition slightly, sailing a little closer to the current? I was not willing to negotiate such an adjustment quite yet, so I applied the slightest sideways pressure to move her back to where she had been and could tell she resented this as she once more shook her head and began easing out across the top of the run.

A gain she begins moving left. But as she passes through the main current she can sense it pulling her backward, and she feels that now even the river itself is working against her. Down she goes, as deep as she can go, until the bedrock itself forces her to halt for a moment, her egg-laden belly brushing the gravel that eagerly awaits the burden she bears.

Her lower jaw scrapes the stones and sends tiny rounded pebbles fleeing into the flow as again she shakes her head in ever-growing bewilderment. Her measured strength is ebbing, and no longer can she maintain herself against the current.

And so she turns, circling erratically in the flow, searching for an eddy, a crease, anything that will give her respite and allow her to regain even a small portion of the strength she has lost.

But now she can sense herself being eased ever upward and backward as the angle of force against her becomes steeper with each diminishing sweep of her broad, fanning tail. She tries desperately to remain upright, but her strength is nearly gone and she is now beginning to lose the ability and even the will to resist.

Then she sees it, a tall, rippling creature towering overhead, seemingly disconnected from her, yet holding her by some unknown force she cannot understand. She feels herself being pulled downstream toward oblivion and tries to give one last surge, away. But she has finally arrived at the limit of her strength, if not her will, and she feels herself being turned one final time, first cross-current and then down, down, down toward the creature that now nearly owns her.

With one last feeble thrust she tries to turn back into the flow, but she cannot. And as she senses the water moving past her upturned side and sees the thing now hovering above, she can suddenly feel the creature beneath her and sees the ceiling of her world receding below and senses a sudden pulling force that stings and tugs at her upper jaw.

And finally she understands.

Now as I write, I once more feel the same sudden chill I felt when I first saw her face. I have never before or since had a trout look at me the way that trout did. Her unblinking gaze was a dagger that pierced my sensibilities, and for one brief moment I nearly stepped backward, away from her.

She lay in my own eddy at the end of my tippet, still on her side, the net just a few inches beneath her lightly writhing body.

And I just stood there like a fool, overcome by indecision.

As I said, I had intended to have this trout. We'd not had fresh trout for a long time, and I had promised Carly that I would serve her one that very evening. And now this trout was looking at me as though she knew I meant to kill her.

Did I mention she had no soul?

I could easily have netted her and postponed the decision for a moment. I could even have let her hang there in the current until I regained my composure. But I did neither.

I still don't understand. It made no sense then and it makes none now. She was a perfectly good trout, and Carly would have relished the meal. The fact is, she and I and Mary Jane dined on trout that very night.

But not this one.

Because I knelt there in the evening flow and slipped my hand beneath her side and lifted her noble head ever so slightly from the water, then carefully removed the embedded fly from inside her upper jaw. I spent a long time with her, working her side to side, her face upstream, in and out of the edge of the current, letting the life of the river replenish her own, and it took a minute or two or maybe even three before she began to writhe once more.

And still I held her, she in the water with her nose pointed upstream and I with one chilled hand held lightly beneath her chest and one firmly around the base of her broad square tail, our two spirits for one long liquid moment still entwined as her relentless undulations expressed her ever-growing desire to be free.

I do not recall the precise moment she left. But I do remember the way she eased backward down the edge of the fleeing current, looking not at me before easing out into the main channel, then turning and disappearing into the dimming dusk from which she'd sprung.

CHAPTER 6

HOME WATERS

"What it was about those times,
I will probably never fully understand,
much less recapture."

At this moment I sit alone on a moss-covered rock in the middle of the Clinch River just a few miles north of Knoxville, thigh-deep on ancient stone. I am somewhat nearer the far shoreline than the one from which I entered this morning at dawn, having just brought to hand and released one more trout of many that over the years have been lent to me by their Creator. She was a brown trout, all fat and buttery with big crimson and ebony spots, and as wild as the river to which she was returned. The water is cold, the air is soft and still, and the late afternoon sun is warm on the back of my vest.

As I look upstream into the lowering sun and then turn to scan the broad bend below where I mean to invest what little is left of the evening, I can see at least a dozen other fishers, some human and some heron, all going about their common task, the nearest barely seventy yards distant.

But this is not their river.

It is *mine*.

For I alone among them know intimately from where these waters spring. I discovered it for myself in distant days now dimly recalled, when as a child I first sought refuge from the world in a pristine little valley in southwest Virginia in the headwaters of this river that now flows around me.

But that was another time and another place, before we moved south to Tennessee. It was a time of innocence and a time of bliss, when the valley at our doorstep was mine to roam to my heart's content, and when for one brief moment I was free and untethered to the world that would soon enough impose its own constraints.

The little brook at the bottom of the valley was still too small to hold trout, but the tiny creek chubs that populated those seminal waters of what would soon become the Clinch occasionally found their way onto the end of my line. It was easy fishing for a child still on the threshold of life, before we left our home in Virginia and moved a hundred miles south into a new land and uncharted waters . . . the waters where now I pause.

The Clinch fishes hard here in July and August. Too many months of sulphurs and sulphur fishermen have imparted a certain sense of sophistication to these trout, elevating them to a point of selectivity beyond all creative reason.

In mid-summer they seem to carry themselves somewhat lower in the current and hold their noses higher than they do in the silly, succulent days of April and May. A well-presented Light Cahill sometimes brings nothing but trout chuckles up from the depths, and a beadhead Prince Nymph sent to probe the depths will seldom produce much more.

Emergers swinging just below the surface fare no better, and at this time of year I sometimes find my thoughts wandering off to the tiny mountain streams four thousand feet higher and the audacious native brook trout they often hold.

But I also find myself thinking about that lovely little stream from another time now long passed:

One hundred and eighty meandering miles upriver from where I now sit, there is a gentle green valley where I would like to think that somehow my childhood footprints might still be found. Down between those hills flows a small quenching brook, and if you follow it far enough upstream, it finally disappears into a dark patch of verdant grass that is always soft and damp and cool and will still soak a child's toes even on the driest summer day.

Above, there is nothing but green rounded hills and sycamore trees and honeysuckle fence-rows, along with one old beech that continues to stand sentinel near the crest of the ridge, beneath whose boughs you can sleep your deepest summer sleep and awaken having momentarily forgotten where you are or who you are or even why you are there. In that valley, deer and rabbits, meadowlarks and redwing blackbirds live and thrive.

And for a time long ago, so did I.

What it was about those times, I will probably never fully understand, much less recapture.

But now as I pause here for a moment in the middle of this great river before rising to continue my evening of bliss, I realize that the farther downstream from that little valley I have journeyed since those innocent days of childhood, the more complex life's currents have become.

And I finally see that in the end we're really not all that different, the trout and me. Sometimes we are predators and sometimes we are prey, constantly grappling with the currents that swirl around us. Sometimes we are content to remain as we are, and sometimes we dare to venture out against the flow.

Eventually we will all die and return to the waters and the earth from which we were formed.

But still the river shall flow.

CHAPTER 7

FULL PLATE

"... no stream had ever come
to me as this one did that morning."

Let's see . . . it was Dad and me, and Joe and the Insurance Man. I can't remember the Insurance Man's name. I think it was Archie or Arcky or Ivy or Icky or something like that. But after all these years I simply cannot remember.

He had an insurance man's name, and his favorite expression, which he used *ad nauseam*, was " . . . mighty fine!"

But now it doesn't matter – it really never did matter; he was Joe's friend, not ours.

Don't get me wrong. He was a nice enough fellow. Perhaps a little loud and a little high-rent, but nice enough. He struck me as someone who was used to getting his way, someone who would always fill up his gas tank instead of putting in just a couple of dollars' worth, someone who would take more than one slice of lunch meat for his sandwich and then nick the last bottle of pop. But we just didn't know him.

We knew Joe. I still remember him. Just like I remember that day. It was a good day, the first day I had ever fished with waders, the first day Dad could afford to buy them for me. We stopped at Ward's to get them that Friday evening on our way up to meet Joe and the Insurance Man on Laurel Fork.

It had rained that morning, and as I tried without success not to stare out the window of Mrs. Hite's eighth-grade English class, I couldn't help but think of how the stream would be running full the next morning, slightly cloudy, with good color and the pools a deep inviting steel and forest green. I really didn't know Mrs. Hite all that well, but she was a nice lady who had once spoken a well-timed and much-needed word of encouragement to me that I have remembered and appreciated ever since. These are really about the only impressions I still have of her eighth-grade English class, along with the day a month later when we happened to be discussing President Kennedy on the morning of November 22, 1963, in those lingering hours of youth when November 22, 1963 was still just another day on the calendar.

But this was October, and Laurel Fork in October was, and still is, a fine place to be and a fine time to be there.

At least this one was.

We pulled up and over the ridge and down into Dennis Cove as dusk was settling, and Joe and the Insurance Man already had camp set up when we got there. The fire was glowing red and orange and was flecked with coral and cobalt blue, so that all Dad and I had to do was pitch our own tent in the waning light and set the grill grate over the glowing coals and dig the steaks out of the cooler and listen to them as they popped and sizzled and eased from blood red to rare.

God they were good, and we told Him so and thanked Him for the steaks and the stars and the silence. And of course for those new waders awaiting their baptism at first light.

The men went to bed around ten o'clock amid talk of an early start and a late breakfast of fresh-caught trout. I stayed out by the fire alone for a long time watching its ever changing colors and patterns as little shots of yellow and orange sparks popped and cracked and then flew heavenward to disappear among the silver stars burning bright against an ebony sky.

It was well past midnight when I finally crawled into the tent beside Dad. I pulled the wool blankets up around my shoulders and my dark stocking cap down over my face against the chill of the night and soon drifted off to sleep to the whisper of the stream and the silence of the stars and Dad's soft breathing mixed with the intermittent sounds of a fire dying abandoned and alone.

When I awoke, *I* was alone.

W arm, diffused colors filled the tent, glowing olive and gold inside my cocoon. The sleep in my eyes and the latent smell of wood smoke were now the only remnant of the night. Dad had let me sleep in, and it felt warm and good as I crawled out of the tent on hands and knees and stood there in the cool open woods, alone and content in my stocking feet.

Soothing fingers of sunlight filtered low through the misty trees and caressed the warm, blue whispers of smoke still meandering upward from last night's dying embers. The entire glade was mine, and I was in no hurry to go.

You have to understand, this wasn't *my* country. It never had been, and it never really would be. We had come here as escapees from the coal fields of Virginia and West Virginia a couple of years earlier, and now the only thing still at all familiar in life was the trout fishing. And even *it* was somehow different.

In the Virginias I had always caught trout. *Always*, without exception. There, I knew the streams, and I knew the rocks and riffles and runs that defined their individual character, and most importantly, I knew the trout and the men who fished them.

Sure, I was just a kid, but I couldn't tell it . . . at least not by the trout fishing. All of Dad's friends had been my friends as well, and they'd always treated me as an equal and not simply like Dad's kid. It's just the way it was back home in Tazewell County, and I had simply taken it for granted.

But here in Tennessee I had trouble catching trout. I fished the same as I had in Virginia, but somehow the trout seemed to have a different point of view, and I still don't understand why. And to make matters worse, Joe and the Insurance Man treated me like Dad's kid. Only Dad was a constant.

And, of course, my fly rod.

Everything else here was different. The mountains, the people, the culture, the customs, even the accents were different, and everyone seemed to have trouble pronouncing our last name. Back home in the ethnic mix of the coal camps, our name was as common as Smith, Hall or Harmon . . . Roydon, Goodekuntz, Dudenbostel or Kovali.

But here our name was strange, and so was the country and so were the people. Now as I stood alone beside the tent in my stocking feet, I breathed easily for the first time in a long time. The morning was mine, unencumbered by the past, undaunted by the present, unthreatened by the future. Just here, now, warm toes in sandy socks with the stream fifty yards away calling to me in vague yet familiar whispers.

There were still biscuits from last night's supper and water in the jars Mom had filled for us before we'd left home, and I ate and drank as I sat alone on my rock, dusting the sand from the bottom of my socks as I reveled in the unfamiliar process of sliding used feet into new waders.

We'd already rigged our fly rods and stuffed what little gear we needed into our coat pockets last night by the fire, so all I had to do was slip on my jacket and cap, pick up my rod and ease down the trail in my new waders. I could tell by their tracks that Dad and the others had gone upstream, and normally I would have followed after them. But this morning was not normal, and I headed downstream into unfamiliar waters.

"You do nice work."

I had heard Dad say it a hundred times to Him who had made all this as we walked the trails and fished the streams. And now for the ump-hundredth time I found myself emulating him. It was already a good morning, and it was enhanced by the two does that crossed the stream below me, heads down as though unaware or unconcerned with my presence.

The new waders were just a little awkward at first. But gradually they became a natural extension of my legs and feet, and I found myself searching out puddles in the trail, leaving them splashed, swirled and muddy in my wake.

It had always been a trying thing, wet-wading these bone-chilling trout streams in nothing but blue jeans and sneakers, even in the heat of summer, for trout require water that is little over half of my own body temperature; it wasn't until many years had passed that I finally realized I had most likely already experienced hypothermia in my blissfully ignorant days of youth.

The morning was easy with its light and its mist and mood, and frankly so was I. The narrow, shaded trail led through a tangled tunnel of laurel, then into an open evergreen clearing in the midst of the thicker hardwoods.

It was here the creek curved back to meet me, sweeping far beneath a veteran hemlock and exposing its roots, creating a deep hole where trout should live. I swept my small streamer across and above it, then gave it slack and let the little weighted fly sink with a twitch as it entered the head of the dark water beneath the undercut.

I thought I saw something move deep in the hole, but I wasn't certain and so resisted the impulse to strike on sight instead of feel. I let the fly carry on downstream and feather upward at the end if its swing, just like Dad had taught me.

On the second drift a trout hammered it. He was so embarrassed, thrashing about in the undersize water as though he owned the place, and when he finally came skating on his side across the surface and into my net, I knew I had the beginnings of breakfast.

And that's the way the morning went. Never before had I fished so alone or so well, and no stream had ever come to me as this one did.

A second trout assured a tolerable meal, and I released the next two before slipping a third into the creel.

I fished my little streamer, I fished nymphs, and I fished dries. I fished the riffles, I fished the pools, and I fished the deep, oxygen-pocked bowls beneath miniature waterfalls and caught trout that morning like I had not caught trout since we left Virginia.

Some leapt, some sulked, and some freed themselves before I could. By nine-thirty it was over.

My empty stomach and full spirit said so.

Moving back up the trail, I crossed a little feeder branch deep in the laurel where I knelt in its cool, shaded edge and cleaned my three trout. I then slipped them back into the creel which earlier I had lined with fern and rhododendron, rinsed my hands, washed my face and headed up the narrow shaded path.

The sweet smell of wood smoke wafted through the morning woods, and I could see Dad hunkered over the campfire as I walked into the clearing. Whenever Dad hunkered, something good was sure to come of it. I think he sometimes prayed over his food even as he was cooking it, and whenever Dad prayed, the results could be pretty spectacular. At least that plate of fresh trout he handed me was.

They were hot and their skins and tails were golden crisp, lusciously seasoned by the cool autumn air and my Dad's own attentions. I ate slowly and purposefully and listened to the percussive crackling of the three trout I had kept as he seasoned them and covered them with cornmeal and eased them into the hot skillet for his own breakfast.

I watched him closely as I ate and even offered him one of the trout from my plate while it was still hot. But he declined and went about his cooking and then his eating with great deliberation.

And when it was done, I knew I had fed from a full plate.

hat's about all I remember of that day. Except for lunch. For as we gathered to fix our sandwiches, I noticed that the Insurance Man took two slices of lunch meat for his own sandwich after Dad and I had each taken just one.

I didn't say anything and neither did anyone else, but I don't think he ever fished with us again. But no matter . . . I was still quite full and content from breakfast that morning.

For that matter, I still am.

Chapter 8

A Good Thing

" The Falls Hole is
the defining run in this stream
that had defined our lives for so many years,
and Dad had learned its every nuance
in decades now long passed."

Snow and rain tracked nearly horizontal, and tiny shards of ice bit into our faces when we turned into the wind as we stood overlooking the falls, a hundred feet below us on this Christmas Eve afternoon.

"This is a good thing," my brother declared. And so it was. Christmas Eve had always been a good thing for us, no matter the lateness of the hour or severity of the weather, especially when there was a grouse or a dog or a trout involved. Or Dad.

"You and I and Dad will catch a trout today."

I don't recall which of us said it, but I knew it was true, even though we had no real reason to believe it. We didn't even know if the trout were still here . . . but still, we knew it was true.

We had caught them here before on Christmas Eve, Dad and I, back when the stream was in its prime and my brother was too little to come with us. Just a few months after the dam was completed, the high mountain lake had filled and covered the low valley streams. Four years later the giant rainbows had appeared in this one high remnant spring creek, reversions to their ancient urges to retire upstream and make more trout.

Summers spent fattening on shad in the lake had made them large, larger than their stream-bound ancestors had ever dared imagine. Dad had been one of the first to find them, and for the few years before the State decided it could manage this unique strain of trout better than God could, the fishing had been a good thing for those few who knew about it.

But slowly and surely the wild rainbows had been depleted, replaced by hatchery trout barely deserving the title, aggressive and able to displace the more delicate native strain.

Dad's last wild rainbow had been caught here and released many years earlier, and we had wondered since if there might be any of the old strain left. Nearly all the summer trout my brother and I had caught in the last few months had carried clipped fins, though occasionally a small rainbow deserving of the name would show up with colors that mirrored the sunrise and whose fins were white-tipped, translucent and pristine. They made us wonder. But today we would *know*.

Today we would catch a trout.

The snow had now changed to cold misty rain, and I put on Dad's old wide-brimmed hat to try and keep my glasses dry. The steep climb down the sodden slope to the falls was treacherous, and twice I had to sit down to keep from falling. When we reached the bottom of the trail, my brother moved upstream a few yards to the large rock that overhangs the Falls Hole while I crossed the bottom of the run and worked my way back up the far side until we were nearly even with each other.

If the wind was only slightly less severe down here, at least it now came from just one direction. Our practiced drifts repeatedly led one another downstream, alternating in the cloudy current, testing differing depths and varying speeds. Thigh-deep in the ancient water, I was better positioned than my brother to fish this run as I felt my way along the rocky underside of the current.

The Falls Hole is the defining run in this stream that had defined our lives for so many years, and Dad had learned its every nuance in decades now long passed. The overhanging rock on which my brother stood was severely undercut, and the swift hydraulic that spun four feet beneath him required the ultimate line control to fish well.

Once when I was a kid I had tried to fish it from where he now stood, but I couldn't manage the proper angle. I smiled as I recalled that day so long ago when Dad had been standing where I now stood and how he had very patiently tried to coach me as I sat up there on the hanging rock. But I was young and impatient, and when I had finally proven my incompetence beyond any reasonable doubt, Dad had fished it correctly, hooking and bringing to net a fat, four-and-a-quarter pound rainbow.

Now I reached across time and the narrow cleft in the current with the old rod, just as I had once watched Dad reach. I allowed no slack line on the surface, barely brushing the rod tip on the underside of the hanging rock just an inch or so above the swirling water. And as I tried to emulate what he had once done, I heard his calm voice behind me above the whispering roar of the Falls.

"You have to get your rod tip beyond the current there, back beneath the cut where the water eddies and the big trout lie. Remember, they're here to spawn, not feed, and this is where they like to lay up and rest before they leap the Falls."

Dad's instructions were easy to understand, but at the very edges of my ability to execute properly.

"What do I do when the current catches my line?" I asked. "Do I lift or do I fish it out? Are there other good lies below us in the drift?"

It occurred to me that I had never fished this run from this exact position, back when we were certain the big trout were here. I didn't have waders then, and the spawning runs always began just before Christmas when the weather was too cold to wet-wade.

"Hit him!"

Dad's command was sudden and firm. It had come nearly before I even felt the abrupt pulse at the end of my line, and I obeyed without question and struck on command.

"All right!" My brother's voice rang sweet above us.

The big trout swirled deep, and for an instant I saw color I had not seen in years.

"Keep your line tight . . . rod tip up."

Dad's calming instructions were firm and familiar and very reassuring. It was nearly as though *he* were playing the trout instead of me.

"Don't let him get too far upstream; remember the rock where we always got tangled up."

Indeed, I remembered it well but had forgotten it, and his reminder was comforting. I was glad I didn't have to play this fish alone . . . it would be okay with him here. Together, he and I and my brother would catch this trout. One of us had said so.

"Take your time; don't horse him. He's a good one."

I moved out and slightly downstream to improve the angle on the fish sulking deep above me. Slowly he began to turn, and I felt him shake his head as he tried to move across the current to regain the depths beneath the hanging rock.

"Give him just a little pressure . . . *there*, that's good . . . he's turning."

I thought of the net strung over my shoulder and asked, "Should we try to net him here or work him down into shallower water?"

"I think you'd do better to just try and beach him here."

Dad had a good point. My 6X tippet was awfully light for such a large fish, and it would likely not forgive a mistake on my part with the net. Besides, the angle was right and the tailing edge of the run led straight up onto lightly sloping gravel. So as the big trout slowly lost his bearings, I very gently pressured him out onto the sand just beyond the water's edge.

Quickly I laid the fly rod down beside him and lifted him back into the water, rinsing his sides clear and then gently slipping the tiny hook from inside his upper jaw. I looked deep into his side glowing softly there in the cold rain, and for an instant I think I may have seen our reflection.

My bare hands, though dripping from the icy water, were surprisingly warm even in the biting wind, and for a moment I tried to comprehend how I actually felt.

I cradled the great fish in both hands, then carefully yet quickly lifted him ever so slightly from the edge of the current for my brother to see. He nodded, and I knew he understood.

S till kneeling in the icy flow, I eased the rainbow back into the water and held him facing upstream, moving him gently side to side until he'd regained himself and was ready to leave.

I stood for a moment, then turned and walked downstream for a few yards, leaving Dad's old rod still resting in the gravel where I had left it.

Looking up into the looming blue laurel and the low-hanging mist, I tried desperately to remember how it had once felt to catch a trout here with him.

But he'd been gone for so long.

Chapter 9

Cole Creek Diary

"I wanted to believe it, just as I wanted
to hurry, to finally find the truth for myself.
But even more, I wanted to fish . . ."

I t tumbles off the east face of Big Back Mountain, leaping and flowing down its rocky course as it has for eons. Dad and I had fished its lower sections when we'd first come to Tennessee back in the early sixties, and many times we had talked about someday fishing all the way up to the big rock we'd heard about that was supposed to give birth to this little spring-fed creek.

But with Dad gone, I hadn't fished the stream for years, and even then I'd never been above the flat nearly halfway up the mountain that the locals called *Frog Level*.

The old gentleman who first told us about the creek had shown us a pale, faded photograph of himself as a boy with his own father, standing with three old coonhounds beside the big granite rock that he said sheltered the little spring that gives the stream its birth. But we knew from experience that he was sometimes mistaken about such places and events, and so we weren't at all sure that this was the true source of Cole Creek.

O n a cool April evening approaching midnight in my fifty-first year, I decided it was finally time to fish Cole Creek all the way to the top. My fly fishing gear is always ready for such late-night or early-morning impulses, so at five o'clock on a crisp Saturday morning I stepped out into the starry night and struck the narrow trail up the mountain as the first faint rays of daylight began brushing the sky at my back.

Firmly focused on finding the big source rock before my day was done, I eased quietly along the darkened trail beside the lower reaches of the stream for the first mile or so as the woods began to awaken around me. I knew these lower waters well from fishing them decades earlier, and when I came to the low and angular rock shelf that holds back the high grassy meadow along the outer edge of a long-familiar bend, I made my first cast of the morning.

had rigged my fly rod the night before just for this run; it was here where I had caught my first trout on Cole Creek nearly forty years ago. Now I swung my little streamer deep along the rock shelf as I had swung it then, and a fat little rainbow hammered it within three feet of where its ancestor had taken my fly as a boy.

The trout pivoted in mid-air and dove deep beneath the edge of the rock and shook its head in vehement protest of the interruption to his morning. When I finally convinced him to join me for a moment, I slipped my net around him only long enough to remove the little barbless hook from his lip and apologize for the intrusion.

The next two trout also came from old familiar runs, one beneath the roots of an ancient hemlock growing along an outer bend, the other next to a boulder that split a seam where the current edged around a shelf of stone that nearly cut the creek in two. Like the first trout, both of these rainbows were around eleven inches, and both were cleanly hooked and quickly released back into this perfect morning, which was now fully mine.

The next three trout came on a #16 green-bodied Elk Hair Caddis, for the creek had now changed from the familiar extended pools and bends that define its lower reaches to more stair-stepped pocket waters, offering drifts that averaged at most only eight or ten feet. Two were rainbows and one was a small brown, and all were fat and healthy. I hoped there would be more browns as the day progressed, for I dearly love the color and character of these fish from little high-mountain streams such as this.

Perhaps I would even find brookies as I worked into the unknown upper reaches of the creek. I certainly hoped so.

Somewhere I passed into virgin territory, at least for me, and now I was becoming the boy I once had been, feeling the same anxious excitement I'd felt back when I had first fished this creek with my Dad, along with the exhilaration I always feel when I find myself alone on new water with an old fly rod. I cast short beneath a dark cut to my left, gave a quick upstream mend to clear the laurel and struck too soon as I saw a swirl of color rising toward my caddis from the depths.

It took just long enough to find and disentangle my fly and leader from the overhanging limbs for the trout to reorient itself to its lie. Easing back into position, I was determined to control my nerves and this time wait for the strike.

M y first cast was much too tentative, but the second landed perfectly, four feet above where the fish had just risen. The little caddis drifted through a tiny dapple of sunlight where I expected the trout to rise, but it failed to appear. And just as I was about to lift the fly from the water, the fish rose daintily at the tail of the run and sipped it in.

I struck lightly but firmly and she immediately swirled for the dark depths beneath the overhang, nearly entangling my leader with the laurel. I prayed she wouldn't jump. Quickly I bowed and lowered my little six-foot wisp of graphite to the left, and in response she turned back into the main flow.

She rippled dark green and crimson in the morning light, and I finally knelt in the stream and tucked the little rod under my arm as I slipped my hand beneath her. I eased the tiny hook from her lip, and as I released her, she slashed the surface with her broad square tail and dove for the depths beneath the overhang.

Still kneeling in the edge of the current, I looked up and around and thought of just how unique an experience this was – to be fishing a stream I had known since childhood, yet fishing it in a manner I had never fished it before. I eased to the bank, leaned my fly rod into a clump of laurel and dug a biscuit and flask of water from my side pouch, then stretched out against an old hemlock and enjoyed a slow, leisurely breakfast and a quick morning nap.

Now the stream began to narrow perceptibly as its angle of decline became steeper, and the character of the water began to make a subtle change as I and the sun climbed higher. I added a little weighted Black Gnat with its hackles clipped to the caddis on a light, sixteen-inch dropper, catching one trout after another as I progressed.

They were still mostly rainbows, but a few more brown trout began to show up, and I wondered again if I might find the little native brookies as I neared the headwaters still high above.

Some of the trout continued to take the caddis, but most of them now took the Black Gnat, and as I moved higher and the creek became narrower, I removed the dry fly entirely and retied the little weighted nymph straight into my 6X leader.

Somewhere morning turned to afternoon and the light began to change, and I noticed the temperature beginning to drop dramatically as the sky lowered and dark clouds began creeping over the ragged ridges above. Mist began to feather the air and my visibility dropped to just a few hundred feet, and for a moment it began to rain lightly.

Then to my surprise and utter delight, the rain turned to snow, and for a few minutes I was enveloped in a classic high country snow shower that lasted just long enough for me to pull my old wool sweater and raincoat from my day pack.

The snow ended as quickly as it had begun, and the sky gradually cleared, leaving the landscape bathed in a rich, golden afterglow. I had continued fishing, even with the falling rain and snow. And now as the sun broke out, the first brook trout of the day took my little nymph deep beside a submerged tangle of roots.

I dipped my rod tip to the surface and applied as much pressure as I dared to ease him out into open water. I could feel him shaking his head beneath the undercut, but to my good fortune I was finally able to work him out of the tangled roots. Within just a couple of minutes he was securely in my net, where I held him until I could work the fly free and release him.

With the sky clearing and the mid-afternoon sun edging toward the west ridge above, the temperature slowly began to rise with the passing of the clouds, and now the brown trout came out to play.

My next two fish were browns, the largest of the day so far, and I slipped them into my creel with eager thoughts of supper when I returned home at day's end.

I continued to climb, fishing as I made my way higher. From this point on, all the trout were brookies. Some were mere fingerlings and some were as long as nine or ten inches, quite large for these high mountain streams. The ridges on either side of the creek were beginning to steepen noticeably, but the angle of the water started to flatten out and the creek began to widen as it bent around the base of a hundred-foot cliff.

Then suddenly I found myself facing a long, open cut through the spine of the mountain, with a deep, inviting run stretching out before me and the afternoon sunlight glinting off its rippling surface.

I stopped and tied on a nine-foot leader and new eighteen-inch piece of 7X tippet with a #16 yellow-bodied Stimulator. After the tight quarters of the last few hours, it was pure bliss to make a long, sweeping cast up through the slot, where the fly eased lightly into the top edge of the run without so much as a ripple and began dancing down the outer seam of the current toward me.

The old brook trout came to dinner like a kid at Thanksgiving, and as I struck he dove deep. He burst high into the air, the spray from his leap backlit by the late-afternoon sun, then headed deep once again, holding tight to the current for all he was worth.

Even from so far downstream I could tell he was a magnificent fish, for the sun that had lit up the spray from his leap had lit him up as well. I began working my way up the left-hand edge of the creek along a shallow underwater ledge, hugging the ragged rock wall at my shoulder as I went, trying to gain every foot, then every inch, of line that I could gather back onto the reel.

Now he turned and began moving downstream. I did not want him to get below me, and so I turned myself and carefully retraced the steps along the narrow ledge until we were once again nearly even with each other.

He found a new lie and held there long enough for me to cross the creek below him and then work back upstream against the outer edge of the current. I came in from below, and when I was in position, I lifted the rod tip, hoping to position him for the net.

For the first time he saw me, and he suddenly seemed to comprehend what was happening and tore away again, back out into the long main run, taking fifteen feet of line with him.

He was by far the wildest, most beautiful brook trout I had ever seen, and his panicked response to his unnatural constraint was worthy of the most ferocious chinook salmon I ever hooked in Alaska. Again he shredded the silver surface of the pool and then leapt so high that he nearly brushed the overhanging rhododendron along its near edge before arching back into the water. I tried to bring him in quickly so as not to tire him any further and was finally able to reach him with the net.

He was still quite fresh, and I quickly removed the fly that hung lightly from his lower lip, all the time keeping him in the stream. I held him there for a minute or more, making absolutely certain he was fully revived before sending him back to his watery lair.

The moment was flawless, and with the afternoon waning I briefly considered abandoning the idea of fishing all the way up to the source of this superb little stream.

But no, I wouldn't give up now, for was this not why I had come?

And so I eased farther upstream and around the bend where I could see that this was indeed the last long run, for here the little creek narrowed once more and began to ascend more steeply toward the deepening late-day sky. I paused and shortened my leader and switched back to my little Black Gnat, for the water had now become tight and narrow.

Moving swiftly and lightly from pool to stair-stepping pool, I continued to fish as I climbed. I could see the north and west ridges converging to a true summit, now only a few hundred feet above, and I knew that the Source Rock, if it was real, had to be getting close.

But *was* it real? Did it actually exist as the old man had told us so long ago? Or was it just a figment of his fertile imagination, a good story to be sure, both for himself and for us, but a story nonetheless?

I wanted to believe it, just as I wanted to hurry, to finally find the truth for myself. But even more, I wanted to fish, alone here in this day of perfection with most of the mountain now beneath me.

The warm evening light and the presence of brook trout made the moment far too compelling to hurry. And so I continued to dip my little fly into each pocket and riffle as I moved higher. Another brookie struck and I missed him, and three runs higher yet another one hit and I hooked him well and played him into a little side pool where I lifted him from the water only long enough to work the fly from deep inside his jaw with my hemostat, then held him in the clear current until he finally realized he was free.

Three more pools and three more trout, all brookies – and now I too am finally and completely free. Even the lateness of the hour is not enough to diminish the lightness of my spirit, and I patiently continue casting as I move upstream.

My fly rod is weightless and seems to do its work all on its own, leaving me alone to internalize the experience. The fly line moves effortlessly, low above the water's surface, close to the overhanging rhododendron and laurel in short, firm, tight loops that cast after cast deposit the fly lightly onto the narrowing stream's undulating face.

The last trout of the evening hits in a little oxygen-rich plunge pool at the base of a two-foot waterfall and then makes the grand tour of the tiny run as he fights to be free.

Not at all content to confine his contortions to his known element, he leaps high into the cool evening air, hanging for a moment in the shadows before arching back into the water. Twice I fail to get the net into proper position, but finally I am able sweep it around him and watch with delight as the tiny hook falls free. I am careful not to touch him, but instead hold the rim of the old wooden net even with the surface of the water for a moment until he manages to right himself. Then I lower the net deep and out from under him and smile as he flashes away.

Still kneeling in the tight confines of the tiny stream, I look around for a moment, then glance up toward the burnished sunset sky hovering close in front of me. And there I see it. A towering backlit monolith of pure pink granite, perfectly haloed by the sun setting directly behind it, and I stand and slip the point of my fly into the hook-keeper of my reel and wade the final forty yards upstream to the ancient source of my dreams.

I slept alone by the rock that night. Mary Jane and Carly were in London, and there was no one to miss me or worry if I failed to make it home on time. I built a small fire and cooked the two trout I had kept earlier over its glowing coals, adding wine and lemon and the few choice seasonings I always carry in my pack. I had a salad of fresh-picked watercress from the spring and drank from its clear sweet flow coming from deep beneath my host rock.

During the night I was occasionally awakened by the soft scurrying of the local residents, some curious, some cautious, some small, some not so small as they eased past on their nocturnal errands and paused to drink from the living water we all temporarily shared.

In the morning I awoke to a coral sunrise, arose from my warm bed of hemlock and spruce, washed my face, dug breakfast from my pack, then slipped a small granite pebble into my coat pocket and turned and fished my way back out to the sunlit world below.

Chapter 10

Trout Fishing
With Uncle Sylvie

"I wondered if Uncle Sylvie was
as disappointed as I was, now that we
might never get to go trout fishing together.
I desperately hoped so."

We flew across Stoney like Death itself, for that is what we were. Then down we bore into the Bishop valley, now shrouded in four-in-the-morning winter darkness and brimming with death and the innocent sleeping souls whose lives we would forever mar once we roused them from their merciful slumbers.

Our lives had been changed already, transformed by a random chance of fate that had placed a distant neighbor on the midnight shift at the new county telephone exchange. It was she who had intercepted the dread news from the bottom of the valley on the far side of Stoney Ridge. Now we raced to get there before the strangers, who wouldn't know how to tell them. My Dad would know how to tell them, for he had been told before.

"The mine has blown up."

The telephone was not quite yet a marvel to me when I was six years old. True, I felt we had somehow overstepped our boundaries when we got a phone of our own, but then I had felt much the same when Dad bought the Ford. It didn't matter that our telephone was on a party line and we received our ring – two longs and a short – right along with everyone else's. The amazing part was that we could actually talk to someone who was miles removed and couldn't hear us any other way.

Now that I think about it, maybe it *was* a marvel.

I really liked talking on the telephone, back before I learned to fear it. I would revel in the mystery of where my voice was going before it reached Granny or Aunt Ruth. They were just about the only people we ever called, for they were the only ones we knew who had telephones too. But it had never occurred to me that the thing might work in the middle of the night.

Awakened by the harsh, faceless rings, I lay there cold awake in my warm bed, piecing together the fragmented, one-sided conversation coming from the front room.

Why would *she* be calling us at three in the morning? We barely knew her. But as the individual words formed Dad's desperate questions, I slowly realized our lives were changing forever as I lay there transfixed in the darkness.

I tried making it out to be a bad dream. I swear to you I did. But you cannot dream when you are six years old, going on Eternity. As I recall, I think I already knew that Uncle Sylvie was most likely dead before Dad ever came in to awaken me gently as I tried to pretend I was asleep, hoping against hope that I really was.

We had been getting ready to go trout fishing for the last few days, Uncle Sylvie and me. The fact is, we had been getting ready to go trout fishing for as long as I could remember, and now I was nearly big enough to carry the pillow case he'd always said we would need to hold all the trout we were going to catch.

You see, we ate a lot of trout when I was little. One night we might have chicken, one night beans and cornbread, the next night rabbit or grouse or squirrel or trout. There was never any perceived distinction between what Mom bought and what Dad killed or caught. Mom made it all taste delicious.

I particularly liked trout, especially the way Mom and Granny and Aunt Ruth cooked it. Mom's fried trout was beyond description, with its delicate flavor and thin crisp tails, taken with her cornbread cooked in the ancient cast iron Dutch oven she had rescued from the old farm on Cruey Hill. No tall fluffy cornbread with trout, please! Save that for the fancy magazines. You must have *real* cornbread with a pillow case full of trout.

Uncle Sylvie and I both knew I would have to carry the pillow case, because he would be carrying the fly rod. It takes a big little boy to carry a pillow case full of fresh-caught trout. Now as we neared the hairpin curve that marked the base of Stoney Ridge, I wondered if Uncle Sylvie was as disappointed as I was, now that we might never get to go trout fishing together.

I desperately hoped so.

Bishop lay dark and calm, and the tires on the Ford cried as we tore past the church at the head of Long Row. There was no color here, not even in the name of the main road. Mercifully, we had gotten here ahead of the strangers. I still didn't understand who the strangers were, only that it was important for us to get to Bishop before they did. Aunt Ruth had just gotten out of the hospital four days earlier and would need her family to be with her when she found out that my Uncle Sylvie had probably been blown up.

All but one of the company houses on Long Row were built the same: two stories, divided vertically down the middle, four rooms to a side with one kitchen, one fireplace and one family each. It felt terribly strange and unnatural standing outside in the brittle mid-February frost calling up to Aunt Ruth's bedroom window, for I had always been able to walk right into her and Uncle Sylvie's house as though it were my own.

The stars burned cold and quiet and bright in the gash of clear, black sky framed by the hoary ridges towering over us, as though unaware that far beneath our feet the earth was shaken and still smoldering. Dad's breath lingered like crystalline smoke in the icy air as his words fought their way up past Aunt Ruth's bedroom window before dissipating in the barren branches above. At first I couldn't understand why he called to her in a whisper, for were we not here to awaken the sleepers?

Now I think I understand.

don't remember daylight. In fact I'm not entirely sure it ever came. I just remember Aunt Ruth. At first she thought that something had happened to her mother. Until we told her. Did I say *"we?"* I'm sorry. I still get confused, even after all these years. It was Dad who did the talking and Mom who did the holding, and I don't much recall what I did. I guess I went for Bobby.

Bobby was older than me and the closest thing to a brother I had at the time. I would not be seven for another six months, but Bobby had been sixteen since midnight. We'd talked about his birthday this past Saturday when he and Uncle Sylvie had stopped by our house on their way to the hospital to get Aunt Ruth. They were both so excited and happy that she would be home in time for Bobby's birthday.

And now, thank God, she was.

Dad stayed only long enough to make certain he wasn't going to have to drive Aunt Ruth back across Stoney to the hospital. I didn't notice him leave, and when I discovered he was gone, I was frightened for a moment before I made myself realize that I had to stay here for him.

I knew well enough where he was. The picture I imagined is still burned deep into my mind: Dad at the head of the shaft calling down to Uncle Sylvie, then the two of them roping the other thirty-six trapped miners to safety, Uncle Sylvie the last man out.

Surely the two best men in the world could do it.

I don't know where all the food came from. Usually if there was an accident at the mine, all of Bishop would converge on the affected home with food and support. But this morning, most of the families on Long Row had someone still in the mine. What do you talk about when you are waiting to find out if you can continue? I wish I knew, because now I can't remember. Perhaps it's just as well . . . please forgive me, this is difficult. You see, it was the *waiting*. Not knowing. Not just for us, but for thirty-seven families. Do you understand?

Dad came back sometime late in the afternoon. He had coal dirt on his clothes and I remember that one corner of his blue pajama top was still sticking out of his blackened and sweaty shirt collar.

He and I made a quick run back across Stoney Ridge to Tazewell to get some things from home. It was good to finally be alone with him, and I think he felt the same, even though I could tell he didn't feel much like talking.

Still, he made the effort to explain to me what was happening and, more importantly, what might happen *yet*, and I know it must have been difficult for him. Man to little man. No punches pulled. I appreciated that.

When we got home, he turned on the television while we gathered the things we'd need. The network news was on, and I suddenly realized they were talking about Bishop. *Imagine that!* Bishop had actually made the national news. For a brief moment I felt a twinge of excitement, until I realized exactly *why* Bishop had made the news.

I watched for a few more minutes, and I think that at one point I even saw my Dad.

I don't remember much about what happened when we got back to Aunt Ruth's that night, except for Bobby walking past me in the crowded hallway, trying so hard to be strong. I wanted badly to help him, but I was little. To this day I have never told him that I heard it when he said " . . . *some birthday* . . . " quietly, to himself.

I'm not certain where I slept that night, only that Mom made sure I had some warm supper and a kiss.

It wasn't until early the next morning that Dad finally came back up the road from the mine, driving Uncle Sylvie's two-tone blue Buick. The house was full of people and they all suddenly stopped talking and turned to him as he walked through the front door.

He looked past every single one of them, straight across the living room at me, and I knew what I had known all along. I tried to be strong, but now I cried as he held me. Most of the people in the house cried – *but not my Dad*. He had to be strong for all of us.

Now the focus changed from waiting and wondering to *doing*. And there was so much to do. Dad and I and some of the men who normally worked the day shift were outside in the yard when the ambulances began trickling up the road.

Slowly and endlessly they came, one after another, for most of the morning. I had never seen ambulances move so slowly. They all looked different from one another, for there was more to haul out of the mine that morning than any single mortuary could handle on its own. One or two at a time they came, all headed up Long Row and past the church and across Stoney Ridge to Tazewell and Richlands and Bluefield. I was glad we were Christians. It was the only hope we had, for it seemed as though every ambulance in the whole world drove past that morning, some more than once.

Even the birds stopped their singing, and the only sound was the low rumble of engines and the quiet weeping up and down Long Row. I think I remember wondering which ambulance was Uncle Sylvie's.

Back when I was going on seven and Bobby had just turned sixteen.

When I was eight, the mine blew up again. By then I took it all in stride, almost as routine, like the cycles of measles and mumps and chickenpox that seemed to come along every year or two. This time twenty-two men died, and somehow that seemed like less.

It took him three more years, but Dad finally got us out of there and became a glass maker. It was hard for a while, leaving the people we knew. There are no better people than coal people. I tried to understand.

I last saw Bishop four years ago when my grandmother died. I took my brother across Stoney, for he had never been to the mine. A young company guard in a clean pressed uniform politely told us we shouldn't be there. So we drove on down past Big Auger and turned around just before we got to Hartwell, and I think we saw our Dad walking along beside the road when he was little.

We may have seen me.

We got back across Stoney around noon, and as we began to change clothes for the funeral, Mary Jane casually asked us what we had been up to that morning. That was the moment when I finally understood:

It was a bright, beautiful, sunny day and the colors of spring were warm and the air was fragrant outside the open windows of Uncle Ed's house. But as Alan began to describe for Jane where we had been, I slowly realized that my own memories of the morning were colorless, with only a faint hint of smoked grey for undertone.

It was then I realized that all the memories I ever had of Bishop were colorless . . . all, that is, except for the embroidered, rose-colored fringe on Aunt Ruth's pillow cases and the fading red carnations hanging wreathed and dying on too many front doors.

A long, long time ago.

– Chapter 11 –

Accusations, Fuzzy Worms and a Pocket Full Of Glass

"I could walk away from marbles,
but I could never walk away from my fly rod."

f I were ever brought up on charges of being a fly tier, there simply would not be enough evidence to convict me. The truth is, most of what I have tried to do in life has fallen somewhat short of total success. But I must say I have kept trying, and there have even been the occasional victories. But precious few of them have resulted in anything enduring.

And so it nearly was with fly tying.

In my extended and oftentimes misspent youth, I tried without success to tie some of the more traditional patterns, or at least the ones we knew worked on the streams we fished the most. My brothers took to fly tying as though it were second nature. In fact, Jack has the unique experience of having caught stripers and bluefish on the Outer Banks of North Carolina as well as a twenty inch rainbow from the Watauga River in Tennessee on the same fly, a chartreuse-and-white minnow pattern he came up with years ago.

On the other hand, my Elk Hair Caddis tended to look like what *I* used to look like with a buzz cut, my Comparaduns bore a striking resemblance to grains of barley, and the best thing that could be said for my Black Gnats was that they were, well, black.

But then there was the Fuzzy Worm.

he Fuzzy Worm was half the product of sheer frustration and half pure luck. It all started with a tail-feather from Ollie, Grandma Cruey's itinerant peacock, who spent most of his waking hours roaming the ridge that ran between Doran and Raven, strutting famously for any female he could find that possessed anything resembling feathers, be it a pea hen, a chicken or Aunt Moselle in one of her more eloquent hats.

The rest of his time he spent chasing *me*.

Why, I don't know, though my early years spent chasing *him* could have had something to do with it.

I carefully clipped a strand of hurl from the middle of one of his long and questionably obtained tail-feathers and wrapped it twice up and down the length of a #16 dry fly hook, over a half-dozen wraps of .020 lead wire . . . I wanted the fly to sink, you see.

It was absolutely the ugliest fly I had ever tied. Everyone who mattered said so, and eventually it was summarily encumbered with the name "Fuzzy Worm," though by whom I do not remember. And though I kept trying to tie it better, I finally gave up and stuffed the few I had finished into an old cough drop tin that Dad had given me and resigned myself to the fact that I had best keep using *his* stuff.

I always did better when I fished with Dad's equipment, and for that matter, I still do. It made me feel good then and it makes me feel good now. Many times he and I each outfished everyone else on the stream, be it man, boy or beast.

But this was back in the days when I kept score, before I fully understood that trout fishing was for real, as real as anything I had ever known, and not just a fleeting passion or a passing season.

Dad saw to that.

Trout fishing was a full-time occupation for Dad and me, back when we were both kids. And even when the season for catching was done, we were still trout fishermen, eagerly awaiting the arrival of the second Saturday in April, dreaming trout dreams and talking trout talk. There were fly rods to be set up and taken down and ferrules to wax and leaders to mend and trout flies to arrange and repair.

Being a trout fisherman was a year-round activity, even though there were plenty of other ways for defining the changing seasons: sometimes it might be a person, sometimes a dog or shotgun, and sometimes even a game, such as baseball or basketball or football or marbles.

And I really wasn't all that good at any of them . . . well, except maybe for marbles.

Does *anyone* remember marbles?

There were actually two games of marbles we played, and each in its own right bore a marked resemblance to fishing that for some reason only Dad and I could see.

The first and most common game was contested in a circle, or at least the nearest thing we could come to it, drawn rough in the dust with a finger or a stick, and often accompanied by plaintive cries of *"No steelies!"* and *"It's on the line!"*

Each of us would in turn try to knock as many marbles as possible out of the ring with our own shooting marble, or "tolley"; *"tol"* for short. Tols were chosen for unspecified and undefinable reasons, as nebulous as color or feel or attitude. The best tols had attitude. Some men are born to be trout fishermen; some marbles are born to be tols.

We would shoot until we missed or failed to knock another marble out of the ring. I always tried to place my best marbles in the center of the ring, for those near the edge were invariably taken out first. Plains game and schooling fish learn this lesson early in life or else wind up being transformed into mere protein and reprocessed into lion or leopard or heron or hyena.

It was as close to gambling as we were allowed to come, and most of our mothers frowned when we played Keepers.

But marbles played in a ring was a rather common affair and bore little similarity to real trout fishing, though there was a marked resemblance to fishing for bass in a farm pond. The other variation, however, was to me a much more pleasant and selective game, more closely aligned with what real fishing in a real stream for real fish was about. We called it *"Chasers,"* and it could be played by as few as two shooters and rarely more than three.

Chasers, like trout fishing, was best done without an audience. The object was *not* to knock your opponent's marble into a parallel universe, but simply to tag it with your own. We each played a single marble, and as the name implies, we simply *chased* each other, shot after shot, until one of us lost his treasured orb to the other's relentless tol.

ACCUSATIONS, FUZZY WORMS AND A POCKET FULL OF GLASS

There were no rings, no boundaries of distance or terrain, and our only constraint was the recess bell or one of our mothers' urgent summons when they thought their little ones were about to be entangled in the foul tentacles of Chance.

But for those of us who understood the game, *chance* had absolutely nothing to do with it.

Like trout fishing, Chasers was an elegant convergence of strategy and stealth, of wisdom and wit. It was abstract, metaphoric reality in its purest and most primeval form, for we who played were at once both predator and prey, fisherman and fish, and many long days and seemingly endless nights were spent secretly agonizing and strategizing over some intricately swirled glass sphere that no longer lived in my denim pocket.

Some tols became legends, belonging to no one but themselves, deciding daily and all on their own whose pockets they'd choose to inhabit. Some of the best tols even had names, and we all knew them, named or not, for we all had likely played them, or perhaps more accurately had been played *by* them, at some time when the chosen tols had chosen us.

Sometimes I wondered who was playing whom, as I have often wondered about a few of the trout that have left me feeling frustrated and foolish as they have magically disappeared right in front of me with what I sometimes interpret as chuckles of derision, as though they were engaged in their own sport and I was the mark.

It hurt even worse when some particularly delectable and famous sphere had started out belonging to *me*.

In the game of Chasers, there occasionally arose that one especially gifted tol that seemed to find the others all on its own. For me, it was a tiny, clear glass, bubble-pocked moon from the planet Neptune, the color of claret, and smaller by a third than any other marble known to man. To this day, I firmly believe that this single marble had much to do with my subsequent propensity for fishing tiny dry flies on 7X.

When I first began playing it, I received some terribly cruel and unkind remarks from my fellow shooters. But I ignored their meanness as I ignored their ignorance of my tiny tol's interplanetary heritage, which was known only to me.

Its diminutive size, immaculate balance, unmatched clarity and intuitive performance was clearly the result of superior and mysterious manufacture, for it would often weave its way between stones and deftly leap wide cracks in the playground to find the opponents' pedigree spheres of glass, often even striking them from behind and leaving their former owners breathless and confused as they gazed helplessly at their defeated treasures as I slowly and deliberately lifted their lifeless forms from the dust and casually slid them into my pocket.

But my greatest trophy by far eventually came in the form of my cousin David's disgustingly common, outsized piece of overused cull, tastelessly swirled with garish, opaque and clashing colors and pitted with crystalline acne from too much time spent in trench warfare. It had claimed the life of many an otherwise noble marble, some of them my own.

When David brought out the big gun, most of us thought hard and long about which marble we would play, for even if we somehow managed to later win it back, it would likely be chipped, scarred and imbalanced from the impact of the Beast.

Still, it was no match for my little alien orb. And when I finally struck it down, a cheer went up that hovered over the playground for weeks – or at least until baseball season arrived. But I was not into baseball, and as my accomplices turned to their bats and gloves, I returned to my fly rod.

ACCUSATIONS, FUZZY WORMS AND A POCKET FULL OF GLASS

I could walk away from marbles, but I could never walk away from my fly rod. It seemed surely to be a preordained gift from God, for it was the very life and energy that He had invested in *me* that I in turn reinvested in *it* and into the flies and fly line it flew.

I considered golf, for it too dealt in distance and trajectory. But what was the point? Golf was too pedestrian and had no heritage of purpose. Trout fishing on the other hand was controlled, beautiful violence whose stake was life itself, both for the fish and the fisherman. When I was fishing with my Dad, nothing else could touch me.

And then I grew up.

But the trout were always there, connecting past and future, and except for one extended hiatus they have been the thing to which I have continually returned. I have usually fished alone, except of course for my Dad and my brothers and sister, and on rare occasions with someone whom I have sensed has similar thoughts about trout to my own. But aside from Carly and Jane and Beth, I had never taken a rank beginner.

Until I took Thom Ashton.

Thom is a saltwater fisherman and a dot.com whiz who had once flown his Cessna over Watauga Lake on his way back home to New Jersey from Atlanta and had looked down and said, "That's where I want to live." So now he does.

Somehow, the subject of fly fishermen came up in one of our meetings, and when he discovered that I *was* one, Thom expressed sincere interest in seeing just what it was all about. We discussed it at dinner that evening, and one thing led to another and Thom eventually wound up with one of my fly rods, complete with an old vest I had not used for many years and a promise that we would go fishing someday.

When we went to the lake for his first fly-casting session, Thom flogged the water mercilessly for the first twenty or thirty minutes. But then he began to get his timing down, and by the end of the day he was actually casting tolerably well.

And so schedules were checked and dates were set and reset. But the truth is, I wanted to wait until September when I knew the trout on the Watauga River would be most receptive. Kids need to catch fish on their first outing, even if the kids are graying like Thom and me.

Finally, September came.

Right on cue, the trout were sassy and fat, feeding as though they were preparing for hibernation. All the occasional trout fishermen were now focused on the approaching deer hunting seasons, and as we pulled into the empty space beneath the Hunter Bridge, Thom and I saw that we had the whole stream to ourselves.

I helped him rig his fly rod and tied on one of the CDC Comparaduns I can only get from my friends Byron and Paula Begley in the Smokies, and that I knew from experience would send the trout into fits of frenzy.

And though the waders I lent him were a tad too big, Thom and I hit the water like troopers and within fifty yards and fifteen minutes I had hooked and brought to hand three sizeable rainbows and one brown trout from around the big log below the bridge.

Thom, on the other hand, spent the first fifteen minutes trying to get his fly out of an overhanging willow tree behind us where it had impaled itself on one of the lower branches. And that's pretty much the way it went for the next couple of hours.

Perhaps it was because we both wanted so badly for him to hook up, but whatever it was I sensed that my friend was simply trying too hard, and I, of course, was over-coaching. I actually began to feel a little self-conscious about the trout I was catching, while Thom, I am certain, felt like he was having a negative effect on my morning's indulgence, though nothing could have been further from the truth.

ACCUSATIONS, FUZZY WORMS AND A POCKET FULL OF GLASS

Finally we met on a sandbank and sat together and shared a small pack of crackers and a drink of water from my flask and tried to joke about what was happening.

"I think I'm just trying too hard."

"Hey, that's the way it was when you were teaching me how to set up a website," I countered. "Remember, I finally got the hang of it. Don't worry, it'll come."

I admired the way he accepted the morning and especially how much he had enjoyed himself despite his lack of action. I could tell that he had a real future as a trout fisherman if he would just stick with it.

And then it happened.

"By the way, I found something here in your old vest." And Thom reached deep into one of the inside pockets and pulled out an ancient cough drop tin and handed it to me.

At first, it didn't register. Until I slid back the lid and looked inside.

There they were, a half-dozen Fuzzy Worms from another time, another age, another universe, when life was simple and devoid of deadlines and hard drives and gigabytes.

I cupped the old tin in my hands and held it up close to my face, and it still smelled faintly like my Dad, or at least like the tobacco he sometimes carried in it when he fished. For one blissful moment life was colored in warm tones of silver and sepia, and I half expected to look across the stream toward the far bank and see Dad casting.

I don't know why I did it. I had never in my life caught a trout on a Fuzzy Worm, and I certainly had no reason to think it would work now. But still I reached over and slipped the Comparadun from the hook-keeper on Thom's rod, attached an eighteen-inch piece of 6X tippet into the bend of the hook and tied an old Fuzzy Worm onto the end of the new drop line.

"There. Try that."

And as I sat on the sandbank, I watched as my friend and my Dad worked their way out toward the current's edge and then marveled at the utter smoothness of Thom's first cast and of the trout that sprung into the air in front of him when he struck, and of the gentle way he played it and brought it to hand and then carefully released it.

And a cheer went up that hovered over the playground for weeks.

Chapter 12

Ribbon of Darkness

"Now that it's all over I must confess . . .
nearly everything we did, we did wrong that day."

Now that it's all over I must confess . . . nearly everything we did, we did wrong that day, and looking back now, it is all too easy to see our mistakes.

We had made them before, unknowingly and without consequence, and so we did not realize the true significance of our oft-repeated errors. But now they are there for us to see, clear and unmistakable as all such errors are from the cold perspective of time. I should have known, should have seen what could've happened, long before it actually did. And so I alone bear the blame.

We were young, Doug and I; but at age 71, Ted was arguably the biggest kid of us all, though he had been a mentor for Doug and me for years, both in business and with a fly rod.

Ted's casts were always impeccable, so fluid and effortless that the canoe would barely move even when he made his longest hauls, which neither Doug nor I could ever equal without major disturbance to the stability of the craft.

It was a grey October morning when we launched, and the sky hung low above the trees, which were clearly on the down side of autumn. It was a perfect day, a day for painters and poets and fly fishers and canoes and clear, cold rivers such as this.

The dam twenty miles upstream had shut off at midnight and would not start up again until early the next morning, and the upper stretch of the river where we put in was flowing low and easy through the cool morning mist. We'd left Ted's car eight winding road miles downstream by a high and rather imposing train trestle that crossed the river from south to north. And though we had never floated this particular section before, we figured that the distance by boat must be roughly the same as by car, or certainly not all that much farther.

This was our *first* mistake.

We launched our canoes in the middle of the morning beneath a low looming sky framed by autumn-hued sycamores, and within an hour we had caught and released seven fish. Our plan was to cover as much water as possible, working along both sides of the river for a couple of miles before motoring back up to my truck with Ted's four-horsepower outboard pulling both canoes. We had done this many times before on other rivers, and Ted's old motor had never let us down.

So after three hours back and forth across the river and having caught and released more fish than we had ever expected, we decided it was time to crank up and begin making our way back upstream. I pulled alongside Ted's old square-stern canoe and tossed him my twenty-foot bow line and stowed my paddle as we prepared to leave. Then Ted gave the starter rope a firm, quick and abortive pull.

The death scream from the motor pierced both the blue-grey mist and our collective senses as it fired up only momentarily before all its internal workings suddenly seized. The silence that ensued was even more deafening as we realized our predicament.

We were at least four miles downriver from our launch site, typically having floated twice as far as we had initially intended, with an old and now hopelessly locked-up outboard and only a vague idea of how far we were above the train trestle where Ted's car was waiting.

This was our *second* mistake, and now we could afford no more.

Our choices were simple: either paddle back upstream against the current, or continue downriver into the unknown. It was nearly two o'clock in the afternoon, the air was shrouded in mist, and we had less than five hours of daylight remaining, with an uncertain distance still to travel.

And so for now the board was set.

To have attempted to paddle back upriver would have been futile. Had I been alone, it might not have been such a problem . . . many times I had paddled my canoe much farther distances and against much stronger currents.

But Ted and Doug were together in a single canoe, and it would have been very difficult if not impossible for Doug to have handled the load alone, for with Ted in his seventies, it would have been more than he could have managed. Ted told us so himself.

You have to understand, Ted was as practical and objective a man as I have ever known, and now *he* made the decision for Doug and me. Our best option, we decided, would be to follow the river until we struck the train trestle.

And so we turned our canoes downstream, found the flow and began paddling.

The first two miles were a relatively straight shot with a strong current carrying us clear to the next bend. Alone in my canoe I quickly pulled ahead, hoping to locate the trestle around the far bend and call encouragement back upriver to my companions.

I wasn't certain how far downstream we had come or how much farther we had to go. I tried to mentally calculate the remaining distance and daylight and convince myself we could reach our take-out point at the trestle by dark.

It was nearly three o'clock when I reached the long, south-sweeping bend. The current flowed strong but narrow as I hugged the outer edge, hoping against hope to spot the trestle in the distance. But a mile below, there was yet another bend, with only wooded ridges on either side as the river continued west.

I pulled into an eddy along the inner shore and waited for my two companions to swing into view before easing forward once more.

The river had us in her broad, meandering web, and the rest of the afternoon was spent much the same: I would wait for Ted and Doug each time I rounded a new bend and then pull ahead, hoping to spot the train trestle. But by six o'clock, and with little more than an hour of daylight remaining, we were resigned to the fact that we were likely in for a night on the river.

By now Ted was getting tired, but he was still characteristically calm and typically realistic with Doug and me. And so in a deep cut where a small island split the river, we pulled into the western shore to look for a campsite before darkness settled, and Doug climbed to the top of the cut to have a look around.

Two miles in the distance, he spotted the top of a silo and the roof of a house and barn. We were certain we remembered this farm from our morning drive into the river where we had launched, and if we were correct, the train trestle should be just a few miles below us.

The mist had now lifted, though the sky was still low and completely overcast, and we all agreed that our best plan would be for Doug and Ted to climb out and try making their way overland to the farm. But we were also very reluctant to abandon both canoes and all our gear, for we knew that the river would rise dramatically the next morning as the generators upstream came to full song. And I also knew that this evening there would be a perfect full moon.

So agreeing on our nighttime strategy and signals, we transferred all of Ted and Doug's gear into *my* canoe, and I set off alone as together my two friends set out for the distant farm, with hopes of getting a ride down to the take-out where they would wait for me.

I turned to look back as I swept past the lower end of the island and spotted my friends as they reached the top of the cut. Below them, Ted's old canoe floated empty and alone in the receding distance, bobbing lightly in the edge of the little side channel, looking for all the world like an abandoned puppy at the end of its twenty-foot leash. For the first time in hours I felt the tension of the long day beginning to ease, for I knew Ted would soon be safe and not have to spend a cold, damp night out in the open. Doug would see to that.

We had made an unbelievable series of mistakes getting ourselves into this situation, but now I felt it was going to be all right.

I made the next bend as dusk settled into darkness.

A full moon on a bright clear night might be a good subject for poets, but not for a lone canoeist on a strange river, because it makes for such terribly harsh viewing. But to my great fortune, this night was *not* clear, and here the overcast sky finally began to work in my favor. For it gathered the moonlight unto itself, then dispersed it across the landscape in a perfect, cool-blue diffusion of radiance that held back the darkness and lit up the night with a soft, even, monochromatic aura.

The wind that had chilled us all afternoon dissolved with the daylight, and the whisper of the river was comforting as it embraced me with the calm assurance that I was not quite so alone after all. Another hour and another bend, and now my eyes had fully adjusted to the light and I could again see far downstream in the soft, muted glow. But there was still no sign of the train trestle.

For a moment I stopped paddling and simply let the current carry me along as I reached into my pack for a small oatmeal cake and some hard chocolate. It was a truly stunning scene that surrounded me, with the cool air refreshing and the sky hovering above the misty landscape.

In the moonlight I could even see the mountains that formed the far horizons as their elegant crests disappeared backlit into the feathered undersides of the low-hanging clouds.

The trees along the shoreline eased past me in the gloaming, a lone whippoorwill began calling from somewhere out in the night, and a doe crossed a shoal fifty yards ahead.

Then I heard it, at first barely perceptible, a subtle change in the tone and timbre of the river. Its soothing whisper began to take on a slight cutting edge that gradually turned into the sound of shredding fabric.

I knew I was approaching some sort of fast water. Looking ahead, I could see the channel beginning to narrow, and the sky seemed to drop away as all my instincts urged me toward shore.

I stepped out onto a shallow bar and pulled the canoe far up onto the gravel. I tied the bow rope to a deeply embedded snag and set off on foot downstream, using my old paddle for a walking staff and resisting the urge to turn on my flashlight, for my eyes were by now so well attuned to the moonlight that I did not want to risk breaking the harmony of the night. A hundred yards below I could see a narrow cut through the bedrock that fell dramatically into a long, open pool. I would have been hesitant to run this cut even in broad daylight with friends and throw-ropes below me, and I was certainly not going to run it alone at night.

I continued downstream on foot, circling through the dark woods to the inside of the run before emerging back into open moonlight. I mentally marked my portage route as I cautiously returned to the canoe, then floated down to a gravel point just above the rapids. I was able to drag the canoe across the thick, sodden grass to the edge of the woods, where it then took me three trips to get all the gear to the calm water below, the last trip threading the canoe itself through the dark brooding trees on my shoulders.

It was a relief to finally be back in the comforting hold of my little boat with the old familiar paddle in my hands.

The next two miles were pure, unadulterated toil. The long pool below the rapids was broad and still, and what little current there was flowed coy and deep and offered me absolutely no assistance. To make matters worse, the surface of the water was choked with long, thick tendrils of undulating and intertwining grass that clutched and clung to the sides of the canoe like ribbons of darkness holding back time. I sought any clear water I could find, but each open lead was quickly closed by the binding grass, and it took nearly an hour-and-a-half to cover less than two miles. The cliffs and ridges on either side of the river loomed high and dark above me, and I was now ready for all this to be over, to simply surrender and admit defeat.

But surrender and defeat were no longer an option, for the only way off this river tonight was the canoe beneath me and the paddle held lightly in my hands and the murky minutes marking each struggling stroke – along with the ever-narrowing focus on something so vague and elemental as a train trestle somewhere out in the darkness.

At last, a half-mile below I began to see some faint reflections of moonlight on disturbed water, and I knew that the slow struggle through the long sub-surface grass was nearly over. Once more, hope began to seep back into my soul as the night breezes suddenly freshened, their gentle chill urging me to dig my wool sweater out of my pack. As I slipped my arms into its sleeves and pulled it over my head, it was as though I were being embraced by an old friend, and suddenly I didn't feel quite so alone. The water began to pick up its pace and the long, clinging grass finally faded into the past.

Surely the train trestle couldn't be that much farther, even with the constant back and forth meandering of the river. I wondered if Ted and Doug had made it out. I wondered if they were waiting for me at the trestle, peering upriver into the the darkness made darker by the

94

lateness of the night. It had been nearly twelve hours since we began, and I was beginning to grow tired, and even the walnuts and chocolate that I always kept in my emergency stash brought only temporary respite from the fatigue.

The night had grown long and the river unrelenting, and I knew that while it had been kind to me so far, it would be terribly unforgiving should I make another mistake.

Still, the scene that surrounded me was magnificent. I couldn't help but marvel at the exquisite beauty and stunning detail of the moonlit landscape as I eased along with the flow. But I knew my concentration must not wane, and I forced myself to focus on the task at hand.

I now had no choice but to keep paddling, sometimes with my face into the moonlight and sometimes head down in the bottom of the canoe. I wondered what time it was. But at this point *Time* had lost all meaning and it really didn't matter enough to set the paddle aside and check my watch; besides, I would have to use my flashlight to see, and I didn't want to do anything to disturb the shadows.

Then, without warning I was abruptly thrown forward as the bow of the canoe slammed into something hard and fixed.

I had nosed into a broad shelf of darkened stone. But with a couple of firm, quick strokes I backed the canoe out and then angled it across the current, hugging the upper edge of the bedrock all the way to the far shore, searching for a way around or through its upthrust layers. But I finally realized that the stone spanned nearly the entire width of the river, with only a few small cuts to allow the water to pass.

Looking forward, I saw there was actually a whole series of these upturned rock shelves for eighty yards or more below me, slicing through the water's surface in broad parallel bands, only intermittently broken by small openings and side-slipping channels not much wider than my canoe. It was a maze of sorts through which I somehow had to weave my little craft.

But the course through the bedrock was in places too narrow for my canoe to fit. And so here in the middle of the river I realized I must carefully, oh so carefully, step out and negotiate the knife edges of the rock on foot as I lifted and guided my little boat over and around and through to the open water below.

I eased from one ledge to the next, then felt my way across the canoe to a submerged shelf, the paddle held firmly in my right hand for a brace and the gunnel in my left. I was painfully aware that I must not lose hold of the canoe, for without it there would be no way off these deep, narrow ledges. And so I paused for a moment and placed the bow rope firmly between my teeth. I worked forward and then back, lifting, guiding, *willing* the little boat through the darkness, trying to balance her weight and keep her from tipping, trying to balance *myself* as I eased from rock to boat to rock . . . careful, very careful, do not fall, not here, not now . . . balance, balance, *imbalance*, slip, catch, slip again, and suddenly I am falling, knowing my canoe is somewhere beneath me; but where, where, *there* . . . and she catches me and rocks with me and I feel the old paddle break beneath my shoulder as she rights herself and mercifully cradles me and shoots me clear of the rocks and out into the open water below.

For a moment I just lay there, secure in her embrace, drifting quietly through the night, carried along by the current that had held me for so long. Finally I sat up and collected myself, then drew the knife from my belt and cut the thick cords that held the spare paddle securely beneath the canoe's cross braces.

But for now I did not paddle. I simply knelt there in the bottom of the canoe, peering into the darkness. The moon was lowering and the sky had begun to lift, and there were a few faint stars now beginning to reveal themselves. All was beautiful and still, the only sounds my own steady heartbeat and the muted whisper of the river and the distant murmur of a train somewhere out in the night.

It took a few seconds before I realized the significance of what I had just heard.

But when I finally did, I turned my whole attention to the sweet beckoning sound of that distant train and the low, clattering rumble of steel on steel as its great wheels coursed the rails that steadily bore it nearer, ever nearer, and then it was just beyond the far ridge and tracking out in front of me, turning and paralleling the river downstream. My eyes lifted from the undulating surface to the still, ebony sky hovering just above the dappled moonlight reflected from the water ahead, intently searching until I saw them . . . *lights*, a mile downstream moving high against the blackened sky, tracking south to north a hundred feet above the now-glimmering water, then disappearing into the ebony night and once again leaving it silent and serene.

I pulled the flashlight from my pack, pointed it downriver, and as we had previously agreed, gave three beckoning flashes. They disappeared without answer and I waited thirty seconds and sent three more.

It was as though there were a giant mirror out ahead in the distance, for the three flashes were immediately returned to me, and I to them, and them to me, and my final two flashes told my friends that all was well here in the darkness.

Doug and Ted were waiting for me by the rocks beneath the trestle as I finally eased into shore. Doug hauled my fully loaded canoe up the steep trail all alone and then returned to help me, and Ted took my paddle and thrust a cup of hot coffee into my waiting hands as I reached the top and turned to look back upstream.

We returned the next day to retrieve Ted's canoe. But the farmer had already taken his tractor out to the river, and the old boat was waiting alone and forgiving next to the silo. He would not let us pay him.

We never floated that river again. But I would like very much to do so someday.

Just to see what it's like.

CHAPTER 13

SONNY AND CARL

" . . . trout fishing was always the constant
that bonded Sonny and Carl as children and
then as men, keeping them connected and able to communicate
with one another in languages that required no speech
and needed no interpretation. "

They had not talked in years. True, words had on occasion passed between them, thick and slow and superficial, and most people outside their immediate circle would never have been aware of the parting. But though they had once been brothers, they'd not actually *talked* with each other for a very long time.

Going into business together as men had been much more dangerous than going into play together as children. Up until a few years ago they had always played together, ever since eight-year-old Carl had proudly carried eight-day-old Sonny home from the hospital, two little brothers nestled together there in the front seat of the two-tone Ford between their mom and dad in the days before seat belts and child safety seats.

Carl had waited for a little brother for years, and I do believe he was prouder of Sonny than even his parents were. At least *he* thought so. But if having a brother had been a new and exciting experience for Carl, it was merely normal for Sonny, for he had no other perspective. And now that they had parted ways, only Carl could reflect on the return of an emptiness he had known when he was singular.

Carl had been a part of the outdoors from the time he could barely walk, and this had always been a matter of great importance to him. Carl was elated when he and his dad could finally take Sonny with them and show him all the marvels of the woods and streams. And he could readily understand Sonny's wonder when they would come across something that his little brother had never encountered. But by far, the greatest pleasure for them both eventually became their fly rods.

Even at the tender age of eight Carl was proficient with a fly rod, and when Sonny was four Carl began to take him along as he fished the creek that ran beside their house. It must have been grand to see them going out together, four years next to twelve, fly rods in hand.

Carl had friends of his own, but he'd rather spend his time with Sonny.

Even when he and his dad would go off alone for trout, Carl eagerly looked forward to getting home to show their catch and tell their stories to his little brother, and of course talking about when Sonny would be big enough to come along with them. And so they grew, sometimes together and sometimes apart. But trout fishing was always the constant that bonded Sonny and Carl as children and then as men, keeping them connected and able to communicate with one another in languages that required no speech and needed no interpretation.

And then they went into business together.

I t must have seemed a good idea at the time, and from what I understand they did some very fine work. So fine, in fact, that when others took notice and wanted to join the venture, the two brothers welcomed the opportunity to expand their operations.

But eventually they were swept up and swept away, and dynamics took over that neither of them could understand, let alone manage. I watched in frustration as they tried to salvage what they had built, and if the truth be known, Sonny eventually lost more than Carl.

And then they were each alone.

Over time, Sonny tried to continue doing what other people, and often even himself, expected him to do. You see, he had this thing he did that made him seem more than he had once been, but that now kept him from becoming more than he was, and for a time he was bound within himself, or at least within the man he had become.

Carl, on the other hand, eventually evened out, the dreams that had once pushed him forward now more or less balanced by the concerns that held him back; he rarely diminished, but likewise he rarely grew. And so he simply *continued*. One day at a time, doing the same work year after year, always tallying more or less even. It seemed to most of us who knew him that he did his work and lived his life in major keys with metered rhyme and ordered verse. But often when he was alone, I suspect he sang quietly and to only to himself, mostly in minor chords and with dissonant notes.

He seemed hopelessly comfortable.

The end of a dream is a terrible place. Sonny kept at it as best he could, for the dream was harder for him to abandon than it was for Carl. In fact, he very nearly never did. And really, neither did Carl, though he went on with his life and appeared to do well. But there was always the emptiness, that shrinking chasm in his soul that Sonny had once filled and that over time became smaller and smaller, until the Sonny that Carl now knew bore scant resemblance to the Sonny he had once cherished.

Carl missed his brother; but with time, the first few years of emptiness tired into a somewhat shallow tolerance between the two and then settled into an unspoken recognition that while things would likely never be the same, at least they could finally talk about matters that bore no relation to anything of real importance.

Then one day they met on the stream.

It was a place they both knew well and had often fished together in years past. It was a few hundred yards below the old bridge where Sonny had parked alone that morning, and a mile or so upstream from the trailhead where Carl and I had started fishing at daylight. It was a beautiful place, a long run along the base of a cliff below a small waterfall where, once when they were kids, Carl had piggy-backed Sonny across the stream to a little spring for a drink.

I honestly think it was a chance meeting, though one of them might possibly have known the other was there. Neither of them were the kind to stay away from the fishing, especially in early spring when life is beginning to thaw. They both knew the water here very well, and I am certain that for each of them the fishing was more important that morning than the baggage.

Both of them had been successful here over the years, and once they overcame the awkwardness of the chance meeting, they each settled into their own method and choice of fly.

But the stench of separation is bitter, and I sensed that it permeated the entire stream that morning, and even the fish refused to participate.

It was highly unusual for either of them to fail to raise a trout. Perhaps it was that old sense of self that made each of them hurry his presentation, or perhaps the stream sensed a disturbance in the flow.

But whatever it was, the awkwardness they initially felt gradually dissolved into a competition of sorts – not with one another but with the situation itself, and I know that Carl at least found himself wishing that *one* of them could coax a strike, if for no other reason than to release the tension. And that's when it happened.

Carl's fly suddenly disappeared beneath a single evidenciary bubble, and when he struck he was utterly surprised by Sonny's exclamation of assent. Frankly, I think Carl had been concentrating so intently on the fishing that he had forgotten his brother was even there.

I watched them both from fifty yards downstream as Carl played the trout. Sonny kept casting casually, though he was actually focused on Carl and was nearly as surprised as I was when another trout suddenly took his own nymph.

A long absent cry of "*Double!*" wafted across the water, and I still do not know which of the two cried it. It may even have been me.

But frankly, it didn't matter then, any more than it matters now. Carl's trout headed upstream toward Sonny, and Sonny's trout pretty much held where it was, and they both played their fish well and brought them to hand and released them together, shoulder to shoulder as time flowed downstream around them.

Neither of them caught another trout that day, but that was all right.

What was important was the cold drink they shared from Carl's water bottle and their supper together up at the restaurant on Route 321 where I ran into them that night, and most importantly, the corner the brothers turned, standing in fifty-five-degree water that was far warmer when they stepped out together than when they had earlier stepped in separately.

I still see them, sometimes together and sometimes individually, either over at Eddie's fly shop or down on Philip's farm during spring turkey season or up on the river below 321. And now each of them seems more relaxed and will easily mention his brother, casually, with no undertone of regret.

And by the way, did you hear about the one that nearly got away?

Chapter 14

Randell,
The Three-Part Dog

" . . . just about any canine not unreasonably afraid
of its own shadow and who is judiciously exposed to water
at a relatively young age can potentially become
a fairly decent Trout Dog."

t is a terribly difficult thing to find a good Trout Dog. A Trout Dog does not have to be of any particular breed or persuasion; in fact, just about any canine not unreasonably afraid of its own shadow and who is judiciously exposed to water at a relatively young age can potentially become a fairly decent Trout Dog.

But there are precious few who in the end can really become masters at their craft.

I once had a Brittany who, when grouse season ended in February, was still reluctant to hang it up until fall. So she would come with me in spring back to the same hollows where we had hunted grouse in winter. Only this time I carried a fly rod instead of a side-by-side, and I don't think she ever fully bought into the program, though I will have to give her credit for her attitude.

But she never could adjust her thinking, for in her perfectly logical dog mind, these little, wet speckledy things didn't come close to passing for a respectable bird.

So she would just drink from the streams and pee a lot.

The day eventually arrived when she came as close as she ever would to figuring it out for herself. We were in our canoe in a little cove off Melton Hill Lake on the first Friday evening in March. The sky was somewhat overcast, but it was unseasonably warm, and I thought this might be a good evening for my four-weight and some small poppers for brim.

And we actually got a few to hit; but as I said before, if Betsy wasn't all that impressed with trout, she considered a bluegill to be beneath her canine dignity.

As I continued to drift and cast, she sulked in the bottom of the canoe and barely looked up when Junior and Son slid to a stop a hundred yards or so across the cove in their twenty-foot, fiber-formed Bass Hawg with its twin turbocharged 200-horsepower outboards, pushing a massive bow wave in our direction. I quickly dropped the rod and grabbed the paddle and turned the pointy end of the canoe into the oncoming tsunami, and once it had subsided I began casting again.

That's when it got good.

I think Betsy actually heard it before I did, the tearing whisper of wings ripping the silky evening air. She was up in an instant and spotted four ducks coming straight for us.

I must confess, this was somewhat of a surprise to me, for in all her dog years Betsy had never expressed any interest whatsoever in the pursuit of waterfowl, though once as a puppy she had given Harley, Mr. Galyon's old grey goose, a good run across the barn yard before he had suddenly turned on her and explained the term "pecking order" in a way that left a lasting impression.

Now, she was past me in a flash heading for the bow of the canoe, where she landed already on point to receive the ducks as they set their wings and lowered their landing gear and skidded to a stop barely forty yards away, chatting discreetly among themselves and casting wary looks in our direction. Still on point and hanging precariously over the front of the canoe, Betsy quivered and whined and threw backward glances at me and my fly rod, imploring me to cast to the ducks.

I could have sold her right there on the spot to Junior and Junior, Sr. had I taken their offer, and for high dollar at that. I would just as soon have sold my one good eye.

That may have been the last time Betsy ever showed any interest in the canoe, though once I bumped it and knocked it sideways in its berth atop her kennel as I was feeding her, and she quietly stepped back into her condo and refused to come out for dinner that evening.

As I said, it's hard to find a good Trout Dog.

The single most disreputable Trout Dog wannabee I ever met, however, was a half-bluetick, half-redbone, half-husky cur named Randell who was owned by (or perhaps I should say, lived in the same general vicinity *as*) my old friend Al Ward in northern Ontario a few miles west of Thunder Bay.

Randell had the sickliest coloration of any mutt this side of Sirius, a left-over product of his unique inbreeding which had resulted in a light grayish purple that I have seen turn much stronger stomachs than mine on first viewing.

Betsy never did like Randell all that much, and she made darn well sure Randell knew it. Al had hopes of turning him into a bear dog, but it never quite panned out. Because aside from his inherent ugliness and the fact that his name was misspelled, Randell had one over-riding flaw you absolutely *never* want to find in an aspiring bear dog: He was afraid of bears.

Al tried him on moose a time or two, but that didn't work out very well either, because the moose just couldn't seem to come to grips with the concept that they were supposed to be intimidated by this oddly colored little fellow-quadruped, and so they would just as often chase Randell instead of running away.

It was quite an embarrassment to all concerned, especially the moose once they realized just what it was they were doing. For his part, Randell had no pride, so he really didn't care; private speculation was that he simply enjoyed the run.

But it was while they were working on moose that Randell and Al accidentally stumbled upon the one thing they thought Randell could do with conviction, infinitely worthless though it was.

You see, with Randell's unique breeding, he loved to chase anything that couldn't have him for supper and wouldn't chase him back. So this was where they began their initial experiments with deer.

N ow the voluminous song of a redbone is rich and compelling, and the eloquence of a bluetick will stack goosebumps on top of goosebumps with its deeply embedded undertones. But a husky is more contemplative and therefore just doesn't have a heck of a lot to say, at least not that he can say all that well.

It is extremely rare to hear a husky bark, and a good modulated *"ooooo"* is about as much as one can hope for, even on a good day with a tailwind. So when Randell was after a deer, a good, loud deep-throated whine was about all that any of us could reasonably expect.

The single worst habit that Randell ever developed was directly attributable to his laziness and his inherent lack of character. You see, if the chase for any deer went on for much more than ten or fifteen minutes, Randell would simply run out of steam, and so he would *tree* the deer.

Now a deer up a tree is an awkward and embarrassing thing to witness, because you know and I know that deer did not become famous for their abilities to climb much of anything except perhaps each other.

Which created quite a dilemma once the deer was actually up the tree, because it simply had no idea how to get down again, especially with something resembling a half-eaten grape popsicle ecstatically whining and crooning below.

So most of the time the unfortunate deer had to be shot to get them down; otherwise, they would slowly starve to death once they'd consumed all the food they could reach in the upper canopy.

On rare occasions a deer, once dispatched, would fall all the way to the surface of the planet. But in most cases their long legs or antlers would get hung up somewhere in the branches on the way down, and we would either have to climb up and retrieve them ourselves or simply cut down the tree.

All the while Randell would be bouncing around ever so joyously with an expression of accomplishment on his little huckleberry face as he whined with glee.

If he happened to tree a deer while out hunting on his own, Randell wouldn't stick around much past suppertime, and so he would leave the unfortunate deer to its own imagination.

Eventually it became a somewhat regular occurrence for one of Al's neighbors to be easing through the woods, hear a rustle somewhere in the trees above them, look up and comment, "Hmmm, Randell must'a been out this way."

So now that Randell had flunked out as a bear dog and the moose would no longer play chase with him, and with most of the remaining deer population around Shebandowan either succumbing to altitude sickness or shifting their paradigm, the only thing left for Al and Randell to try was fishing.

The first time Randell tried to retrieve a walleye he wound up with a severely perforated mouth from chomping down too hard on the fish's needle-sharp dorsal fin, and he didn't even try to make friends with northern pike once he saw their hideously toothy smile and realized *they* were probably more likely to retrieve *him* than the other way around.

So about all that was left was trout.

And Randell took to trout like . . . *I'm so sorry* . . . a fish to water.

Literally.

For once Al and Randell worked out what I must admit was a rather ingenious method for him to actually *spot* the trout, he would jump right in after them, water and fish retreating around him like the Red Sea from Moses as he splashed wildly about with a confused expression on his disgusting little face, wondering where the heck all his new friends had suddenly gone.

Oh, I tried to reason with Al that if he would just stop duct-taping those silly polarized sunglasses to the base of Randell's muzzle, that Randell would have a harder time seeing the trout through the surface glare and maybe wouldn't be so quick to jump in after them.

But Al stubbornly insisted that without the polarized glasses, Randell was absolutely worthless as a Trout Dog – which was exactly my point all along.

For better or for worse, Randell's outdoor career finally came to a sudden and ignominious end during one of his wider swings, which had taken him all the way to the outskirts of Thunder Bay. To this day Al swears it was merely an unfortunate and completely unintended coincidence of timing, but at that very moment the circus just happened to be packing up and heading to Edmonton. Seeing such a uniquely colored dog showing such intense interest in the animals that were being loaded for the long trip west, some young, well-meaning roustabout packed Randell up with the other critters.

The last we heard, Randell had made himself right at home with the rest of the clowns and actually fancied himself to be a fully functional member of the big show.

Understanding the dog's inherent itinerant tendencies as well as he did, Al had earlier made certain that Randell's name, address and probation number were engraved in brass on his collar in anticipation of just such an occurrence.

He told me later that after a few weeks, the circus manager called from somewhere down around Bismarck with the rather ludicrous offer that for $750 he would put Randell on a bus and send him straight home – and even pay the fare himself.

In his very best Canadian, Al retorted that $750 wouldn't even come close to what it would take to finalize a deal such as this, and so he courteously but firmly declined the offer – whereupon the circus manager offered him an even thousand.

But my friend Al is a wise man; he knows when to accept things as they are and simply be grateful.

Chapter 15

A San Juan Interlude

"It is at moments such as these that the trout
seem to become a lesser player in the greater reality,
at least until you actually begin fishing for them."

To the more seasoned and weathered fly fisherman, it is no longer quite so important how many trout he actually catches. For it is not the *catching* but the *fishing* that matters most, and of course the wild and beautiful places the trout inhabit. For me, one such place begins with an undulating two-lane road that leads from the Aztec Ruins out to Navajo Dam and the headwaters of the San Juan River in northern New Mexico.

Here, jackrabbits and cottontails scurry back and forth across the sun-cured pavement, and when you get out to where you can overlook the cottonwood flats below the dam, a little mule deer buck emerges from the evening shadows and cautiously looks up at you, his forks still forming in velvet. The cliffs around you seem to breath and glow warm from within as they catch the last rays from the evening sun, bathing you in their own late-day aura. An old Navajo man once told me that the rocks here are actually alive. I'm not entirely certain whether he was serious or not, but after experiencing them for myself, I think I believe him.

On the map, this road is just a dark, rather innocuous and twisted little line with highway number 173 printed over it in black. But the map does not tell you what lies on either side of this line or that the road itself is over 7,000 feet in elevation and that it is one of the most spiritual strips of narrow tar and gravel you'll ever encounter.

It leads you out past Skull Rock and Eagle Mesa and Gretchen's cabin and deep into the very soul of the high, quiet desert that surrounds you and embraces you with the pure color and texture of the sky and ancient stone that continually reflect other, more seasoned realities far beyond our common experience.

The map does not tell you that once you leave the gravel and begin climbing north on foot into the high canyons or when you head out onto the broad desert shelves of stone and sage to the south, you are likely to encounter the Grand Process of creation-and-evolution itself still in progress, and may in the end even come face to face with yourself.

Here, the rocks along the skyline and high up on the canyon walls teeter on the edge of collapse as they have since long before Christ last walked the earth, and they will likely be teetering here still when He returns. It is at moments such as these that the trout somehow seem to become a lesser player in the greater reality – at least until you actually begin fishing for them. It works much the same back home on the Watauga or Laurel Fork or Doe Creek, or up on the little brook trout stream where the snow monster lives.

It is the fishing that leads me to these places and that led me yesterday to the land east of Dulce where I met Mrs. Cora Gomez, a kind and beautiful Jicarilla Apache woman whose character and grace resides deep within, a perfect complement to the grandeur and spirit of the land of which she is so much a part.

When Cora speaks, we all listen. For seventy-four years she has walked this land, the last six without her beloved husband, Frank.

In her younger years she spent one long, cold winter in a tent with her little niece Carolena because, as she told me, " . . . there wasn't any place else to live."

But they were fine, so long as Cora had her rifle; her biggest challenge turned out to be keeping little Carolena in coloring books and crayons.

Cora remembers having her mouth washed out with lye soap and then being put into a broom closet by the teachers when she was seven years old for daring to speak her own language, and then proudly counting the nails inside the closet – in *Apache*.

She has taught me to make *biscochitos* and *frybread*, and then how to say "frybread" in Apache.

It is the fishing that led me today to the searing sandy path beside the San Juan where an eagle perched backlit on a precariously balanced rock high along the skyline and scolded me as I walked the hot, one-hundred-degree trail far below in chest waders, while the river flowed cool and unseen less than fifty yards away through the cottonwoods.

It is the fishing that leads me from this place at first light into still higher and much greener country eighty miles to the east in the mountains above Chama, where the streams and lakes are bound by verdant greens and summer golds, in marked contrast to the dry ochres and mauves and cerulean blues found here in the desert, and where my spirit is bound by nothing.

And it is the fishing that awakens me gently in the darkness from an otherwise sound and dreamless sleep to write these things while they are still fresh and alive. For the writing is like the fishing: you take it when it comes or it goes away without you, and it does not come back.

Carly understands.

Meanwhile, I live this life and dream these dreams, and often they are one and the same and it is difficult to separate them. But then why should I ever *want* to separate them? For the fishing I love and the life I live and the things I must do all seem to mingle and intertwine into one great yet fleeting experience I loosely perceive as *life*.

And so I look forward and I look back and I look all around and then proceed without caution or apology into the unknown, where life becomes what it will on its own terms. And there is not all that much I can do except keep pace as best I can and revel in the curiosity of where it may lead.

And did I mention the trout?

CHAPTER 16

THE QUESTIONABLE HISTORY OF THE FUZZY WORM

"For all the years of its questionable history,
it remains the single most homely and disreputable
fly ever conceived by the mind of man.
But it catches trout."

As I sit here tonight in Gretchen's cabin eating my sandwich and grapes following my first afternoon of fishing the San Juan River, I look up at the wall above me and see a painting of the Texas Hole. There is a driftboat in the painting where this afternoon there was a driftboat anchored out along the tailing edge of the current, and there is a fisherman working the run where I caught the big rainbow. In the painting it is dusk, as it was this evening when I caught the big trout, and I can see the funnel upriver where earlier I stopped casting to watch the mule deer doe and the little forkhorn cross the river. I still smell of Deet.

The San Juan is different from any river I have ever fished, and it is simply not realistic for me to think I might figure it out in the couple of days I have to spend here before heading up into the high country above Chama, two hours to the east. I am clearly fishing it differently than anyone else I saw on my initial foray this afternoon.

Earlier, on the way up to where the tailwaters begin, I stopped along the road overlooking an S-shaped bend where the river swept in toward me a hundred feet below, and I met a man coming up the steep, narrow trail. I told him I was from Tennessee and that I had never fished here, and he showed me what he called a "San Juan rig."

It consisted simply of a strike indicator followed by eight feet of gossamer tippet leading down to a tiny copper-colored fly he called a San Juan worm.

The fly was nearly the same hue as the surrounding rimrock, with a foot or so of even more delicate tippet material extending from the bend in the hook and leading back to a dark little fly so small as to be virtually non-existent.

"I have lost four of these rigs in the last two hours," he said, not really complaining.

I could certainly see how.

People here seem to be fishing these full-length rigs with high rods and making long, lingering drifts, while holding their heads at different angles than I do. But given the short period of time I have to be here, it seems beyond my ability to learn quickly. So I will fish for fun and try to fish well and fish the San Juan as I do the Watauga back home, with the flies I know and trust.

So far, these flies have never let me down, whether on the Upper Delaware in New York or the flat sandy rivers in Michigan or the tailwaters and mountain streams of home. Especially the Fuzzy Worm.

What an improbable little fly, the Fuzzy Worm. For all the years of its questionable history, it remains the single most homely and disreputable fly ever conceived by the mind of man. But it catches trout. You don't have to believe me; just ask Thom or Alan or Ben. Alan and Ben are especially accomplished in the art of fly-tying, but even on a good day with favorable breezes the flies I tie are pretty much bottom of the barrel and we all know it.

So it's a mystery to us all why this thing works so well.

A few years ago, after catching way more than his share of trout on the Fuzzy Worms I had given him, Ben finally talked me into showing him how I tied it. For try as he would, the trout simply wouldn't give the Fuzzy Worms *he* tied the time of day, though I had shared the recipe with him before.

So late one afternoon on a visit to his office, I slid my little fly-tying box into my briefcase, along with a couple of #16 long-shank hooks, a strand or two of peacock hurl, a spool of lead wire, and a bobbin filled with mahogany thread. Ben and I sat down at his desk, and as he watched intently, I tied one up in about four minutes.

With the fly completed, Ben looked over at me with an expression of sheer amazement and then calmly pronounced, "There is not a single thing you just did that you did right." He then removed the Fuzzy Worm from the vise, and with a sneaky smile and a knowing look in his eye he took an envelope from his desk drawer and carefully placed the fly inside, sealing the flap with a lick and a grin, as though he clearly had big plans for it.

It was the nicest thing he could have done.

And now as I sit back here at the cabin above the San Juan, battered and burned following my afternoon on the river beneath the high desert sun, I cannot help thinking of the trout I caught today on the Fuzzy Worm.

They're all still up there, wandering around in the river, shaken and confused and trying to explain to their compadres the marks along their cheeks and gums. "Never saw anything like it," they moan. "The darn thing looked so bad that it *had* to be real. No self-respecting fisherman would be caught dead using something that ugly. You don't understand! *It wasn't my fault!*"

I feel especially bad for the two fish who are swimming around tonight with the flies still stuck in their faces like little ugly trout warts, there for all their neighbors to view. Perhaps by now the word is out and other trout are coming from up and down the river to see for themselves, either to make sport of their unfortunate companions or simply to try and learn something.

And I imagine that all along the San Juan, word is spreading about this out-of-state intruder who has somehow slipped past security, and trout mothers everywhere are scurrying to herd their precious little ones into safer waters.

Or not.

We'll see tomorrow.

Chapter 17

Water in
Desert Places

"... in the dimming shadows it wasn't until he
was actually in the net that I could see he was a rainbow."

Y ou can always follow water, whether it still runs free or is merely a latent image left behind in some dry, desert place. From trickles to brooks to streams to torrents, water always runs down to its true source, there to be gathered into the air like so much brood and returned on the wind to the places where it once more becomes trickles and branches and torrents and streams.

Even when water has already run its course and is gone, as it so often does here in the high New Mexico desert where I awoke in darkness an hour ago, you can still follow its desiccated trail.

It's empty path leads up from the cottonwood flats along the San Juan River and then out across the broad piñon- and-rock-laced steps toward the base of the cliffs towering far above as you follow the dry, sandy watercourse higher and higher and revel in the morning being born around you – which is what I am doing at this very moment as the cool blue, pre-dawn desert light hovers in a breathless balance between darkness and dawn.

I n a place such as this, one is small; yet small is a good thing to be. For only by being small can you come and go from the holy places without intrusion, without disturbing or being disturbed, without being obtrusive.

Only when you try to be large do you no longer fit your insignificant niche and declare to all around you, man and beast and flower and juniper, that you are in fact an intruder and therefore neither belong nor deserve to be here.

But if you can somehow *learn* to belong, there comes an evanescence to your spirit you might otherwise never know. The air and the land and the places where once the water flowed embrace you and seed your spirit with their own sanguine essence, revealing a part of themselves you could otherwise never experience.

Then, in a moment of crystalline clarity and with a deep and abiding sense of the present, you suddenly recognize the perfect order that resides in the chaos that surrounds you, and you sense the utter realism of the fantastic.

The air is dry and clear here this morning as the world awakens around me, and for now at least it is relatively cool, offering a fleeting counterpoint to what it will be in just a few hours as the early August sun overruns the day and once more warms it to the point of oppression, when even the rocks will groan in the relentless heat.

Everything here that is alive, from the small desert lizards and skinks, to the songbirds and jackrabbits and mule deer, to the least little flower and cactus and bee, deserves the utmost respect simply for living and growing and singing and buzzing in a place such as this. I feel humble to be a part of the overwhelming silence that surrounds me, if only for this single mystical moment. An eagle is calling in the cliffs above.

This is most assuredly a holy place.

Now as I climb the steepening slope and weave my way among the rocks and boulders, making my way up along a knife edge to the vertical base of the dry cliffs, the crown of the rising sun suddenly dazzles the ragged edge of the sky along the rimrock high above, searing itself into my vision.

I turn away, and far below on the distant desert floor I can see my own insignificant shadow, and I watch in awe as the mountains eighty miles to the west come alive in the low light of dawn.

I have no particular destination in mind as I climb; I simply want to experience the beginning of this day in this place where I have never been, this place for which I have no prior point of reference, this place that is not mine but is even now etching its essence into my soul.

This brief three-day interlude along the San Juan has been different from any other trout fishing I have ever experienced. On the first evening, after I got Jane and Carly settled in and they met my friend Gretchen Lee who owns the little cabin where we are staying, I headed alone upriver to the Texas Hole.

The Texas Hole is arguably the signature run on the upper San Juan, and it was here where I intended to first set foot in the river. But there were too many fishermen already there, some in the main channel and some waiting in line for their opportunity to work the choice spots. The early afternoon air was warm but surprisingly comfortable with its lack of humidity.

I found the only run I could see that wasn't teeming with fishermen and went in alone upstream above the island. As I stood there rigging my standard Tennessee pairing, a CDC Caddis with a Fuzzy Worm dropper, I saw a trout rise in the flat water in front of me.

On my fourth cast he hit the Fuzzy Worm, attacking it as though he had never seen such a strange morsel. His size was small but his enthusiasm was high, and I released him with a smile as I realized he was my first trout from the legendary San Juan. A few casts later I caught another one on the same improbable little fly, a rainbow like the first.

Both trout were about eleven inches long and noticeably lighter in color than our trout back home. I wasn't sure whether this was just an aberration or indeed the normal coloration of desert trout.

I could still see fish taking something from the surface, so after fifteen minutes I changed the little CDC Caddis to a #18 Parachute Adams, retying the Fuzzy Worm dropper two feet below it, then crossed the run, where I took a small brown trout on the dropper.

It was clear that whatever they were taking was not adequately represented by anything I had shown them so far, so I searched my fly box for something, anything, that might work. But in the end I settled on my little nymphs.

With dusk approaching, I chanced to look downriver into the main run of the Texas Hole and saw that it was suddenly and surprisingly nearly empty of other fishermen, and I quickly moved down to where the two channels converge.

I tied on a new piece of 5X tippet with a weighted Carly-22 and trailed the Fuzzy Worm below it on three feet of fresh 6X, then cast slightly upstream and immediately threw a big looping mend even higher. At the end of the drift something significant tapped the line, and I struck too hard and broke off the entire rig.

He had clearly hit the top fly, so I retied the same two-fly set up. Three casts later another fish again struck about halfway through the run, and this time I did not overtax the little three-weight on the strike and everything held.

The trout flailed the surface in the waning light and then burrowed deep, heading cross-current and slightly upstream. I moved directly into the run, then down to my left to stay below him, and in the dimming shadows it wasn't until he was actually in the net that I could see he was a rainbow. I estimated him at close to twenty inches, and even in the dusky light he also seemed to be very pale in color.

As I released the fish, I realized that the few remaining fishermen had left and I was completely alone in this lovely run on this classic river, with the evening entirely mine. For a moment I slipped my bottom fly into one of the rod guides, looped the long leader back around the reel, and just stood there bathed in the fading glow from the warm cliffs above.

This one big trout made the entire trip worth the effort. I was very pleased with the evening, having had these last few moments alone for my first foray on the San Juan. When I returned to the cabin an hour after dark, Jane and Carly and Gretchen and I sat outside and had our supper and marveled at the clear, moonless sky and the millions of stars that vaulted the heavens from horizon to horizon.

I n the morning we leave Navajo country, heading east and north into the land of the Jicarilla Apache, then up into the greening mountains and headwaters of the Brazos where our friends Pat Carpenter, Terry Tiner and Frank Simms are waiting for us at Chama. But for now I have one more day to explore the San Juan.

And as I sit here alone at the base of Eagle Mesa in the soothing glow of the high desert sunrise, I can see our cabin a mile or so below to the south, and far beyond it are the green, meandering cottonwoods that flank the river.

Two small figures, one in pink and one in green, just walked out and sat down in front of the cabin, and I think the one in pink just spotted me and waved.

Breakfast must be ready. And so am I.

CHAPTER 18

GIFTS OF THE HIGH COUNTRY

" . . . the trout were not only stunning,
they were strong and healthy and ready to play,
and life was elevated to new levels
that evening at 9,000 feet."

T he Brazos gathers itself just below the redrock boulder beneath whose upper ledge the big trout lie. Here at the confluence of its West and East Forks at 9,000 feet in the mountains of northern New Mexico, the fabled stream starts its 1,200-mile journey to the Gulf of Mexico, flowing through deep, rock-rimmed canyons and across broad, overlapping meadows, its runs and riffles holding storybook trout of which dreams are dreamed.

I had once lived those dreams, and for years I had dreamt of living them again. Likewise, I knew the names of many of the storied streams of the West and had on occasion actually fished some of them. But rarely had I been able to fish where I wanted to. For other anglers knew their names as well, and the choice runs were often taken once I got there and I would have to wait my turn or look for an opening that all too often never materialized. *You* know how it is. You've been there too.

But I had tasted the Upper Brazos before, it's high-country isolation and strictly limited access maintained by people who fully understand that fly fishing for trout in a place such as this is a sublime experience, one to be savored within yourself or at most shared with a precious few.

To that end I had promised Jane and Carly that someday I would bring them here and let them taste it for themselves. You know *Someday*, that illegitimate imposter who often tantalizes but remains just out of reach. I had chased *Someday* for years, but now as we approached the waning months of Carly's adolescence, she still hadn't tasted the high country of northern New Mexico that had so long ago seduced her father.

I could not for the life of me understand how my six-year-old little girl had suddenly turned sixteen. Carly had caught her first wild trout on a dry fly when she was eight, her little make-believe animals and figurines tucked safely away in her fishing vest, there for when she was ready to play with her own toys instead of mine.

128

She would build entire worlds there along the laurel-lined streams, and oftentimes I would set my fly rod aside and play there with her. But as she grew, likewise waned her desire to tag along with her dad, and her toys gradually became more mature as she discovered wings and fins of her own, just as I had always prayed she would.

But finally we had come here together to fish the Brazos, along with the Poso and its headwaters, and even a few high-country lakes, all of which my surrogate brother Frank Simms had promised me, *swore* to me, held New Mexico browns, brookies, rainbows and cutthroats that would relegate our Tennessee trout to "also ran" status.

"Au contraire, my tall lanky sidekick," I had protested. "It certainly will take more than a few fish with a western drawl to relegate our hillbilly browns, brookies and rainbows to a position beneath your cowboy cutthroats."

This has been an ongoing point of discussion between Frank and me for years. Still, I couldn't resist taking my friend up on his offer, and by early August my wife and daughter and I were pulling on waders by the Brazos.

As president and general manager of the 36,000-acre Lodge and Ranch at Chama Land and Cattle Company, Frank had asked longtime friend Terry Tiner to accompany us up into the high country and across into the valley of the Brazos. Our ride up and over the divide and then out onto the broad expanse of the high valley was enhanced by sightings of elk, mule deer, turkeys, blue grouse, bobcat and one truly magnificent cinnamon bear.

Still, it was the *trout* we had come for, and as we stepped into the stream and Terry and I were explaining to Carly and her Mama just how this was supposed to be done, my dear little daughter had the temerity to interrupt us in mid-lecture by hooking the first trout of the trip.

It was a classic twelve-inch brookie which she played to perfection and brought to Terry's net, then posed for the obligatory photographs like she had somehow done this a few hundred times before, which in fact she had back home in Tennessee.

Now that we were officially into the program, I looped a Dave's Hopper into a lovely little riffle and let it sweep down-current into the shadows beneath a large boulder a few yards upstream from where Carly's trout had just hit. It disappeared with a liquid thump that took my fly deep into the dark water beneath the ledge.

He was an incredibly strong fish, and as I began to better appreciate Frank's point of view, Terry slid in below me, and after a couple of minutes of intense negotiations with the brookie, we finally brought him to net. He was an eleven-inch masterpiece from whose jaw I slipped the hook and then eased him back into the stream.

And that's pretty much how the morning went, one beautiful brook trout after another, with enough rainbows scattered into the mix to keep us on our toes, until even Jane had to take a turn with the net while Terry was helping Carly change flies. We knew of course that the browns would come, and later there would be the newly reintroduced Rio Grande cutthroats. The days ahead held great promise.

Terry called us back to the truck for lunch sometime around noon, complete with sandwiches and salads and desert, all served from one of the lodge's signature wicker picnic baskets on a fancy, red-checked table cloth laid carefully across the tailgate, clearly a concession to the ladies in our company.

After lunch, with the brookies and rainbows still fresh in our minds, we would head even higher, all the way up to the tiny headwaters of Poso Creek where Terry and Frank had promised we would find the Rio Grande cutthroats.

This is a rare little trout, once native to these waters but long since displaced over much of its original range by the more aggressive rainbows and brookies. But when the state of New Mexico had determined to reintroduce this species into its proper habitat, the folks at Chama had eagerly embraced the concept. Now these trout were living happy and productive lives somewhere out in the high country meadows, which after an hour's trek spread themselves before us.

Afternoon breezes rippled the broad, multi-hued expanse of swaying grasses and wildflowers for as far as the eye could see, or at least until they merged with the black timber that rose to the skyline. But darned if I could pick out anything that even remotely resembled a trout stream.

Still, Terry headed off into the high grass, and determined not to be outdone, we followed him as though there might actually be living water hiding out there somewhere. And sure enough it was there, not a creek but a diminutive little trickle that I swear was not more than eighteen inches across.

Incredibly, Terry declared we would start fishing right here.

At first I suspected that he and Frank had set me up for this, just to see if I would fall for it. Then as I was trying to decide whether to be a good sport and play along, Terry's rod tip suddenly dipped toward the water like a dousing wand and he was hooked up.

The fish he brought to hand was unlike any I had ever imagined, and the edges of my perceptions began to crumble as I tried to come to grips with the little trout's elegant hues and intricate patterns.

It began beneath its lower jaw with two signature slashes of scarlet that give the cutthroat its name. But then it were as though someone had plugged the fish into a power source and flipped a switch, for its colors seemed to effervesce from within. The depth and iridescence of its blaze-orange gill-plates was framed in perfect counterpoint with vivid kelp greens and deep royal blues, all intermingled with subtle mauves and purples. The parr markings along its sides floated steel grey and bronze and pale amber against a tawny field of gold-flecked scales, with eloquent gestures of coral edging its ivory underbelly. This symphony of color was finally brought to a crescendo by an elegant sweep of oversized ebony orbs beginning high along the dorsal fin and then patiently building to a perfect finale along its tail.

I had never imagined there could exist such a trout, and I nearly had to sit down right there in the meadow to regain my composure. I looked into the marled, sun-dappled water, and as I watched Terry carefully revive and release the fish, only then did it occur to me that I might be able to catch one of these treasures myself.

The next few hours were one of those timeless interludes with which every life should be adorned, one that forever richens your memory, to be brought forth and savored in life's less kindly moments. There were places along the stream that were actually wide enough to make a decent cast, and places where we had to lower our flies vertically down through the slot between the tall, leaning grass growing on either side of the flow, then lay it gently onto the surface of the water and hope for a five- or six-foot drift if we were lucky.

And we *were* lucky. And we were blessed, for the trout were not only stunning, they were strong and healthy and ready to play, and life was elevated to new levels that evening at 9,000 feet.

I love ending a day in such a rarified atmosphere; there was certainly nothing more we could do here that might possibly make the day any more sublime. So as Jane and I followed Terry and Carly back to the truck, I lingered behind to photograph the sunset as coyotes began singing a perfect ending to a perfect day. And that night, following a gourmet five-course dinner and with Jane sleeping peacefully beside me, I savored the day just lived and the days still to *be* lived and then drifted away amid dreams of daylight.

Dawn finally sifted into our bedroom and nudged me awake. I showered and dressed as quietly as I could so as not to disturb my sleepy friend and made my way down the long hallway and out into the greatroom to breakfast. Jane and Carly would sleep in this morning and then invest the day enjoying the amenities of the 27,000 square-foot lodge. I was leaving them in good hands with Frank, who was characteristically smug this morning after hearing about our previous day's fishing.

Likewise, for the moment I didn't have a heck of a lot to say about our Tennessee trout as Frank and I sat together and ate breakfast. When Terry joined us, I finished my last sip of cowboy coffee and we were off, just Terry and me along with our fishing gear, and Frank of course doing his very best *Meanwhile Back at the Ranch* number, comfortably in charge of the ladies.

"We'll hit the lakes first thing this morning if that's okay with you," Terry suggested as we stowed our gear in the ranch truck.

"Hey, that's your call," I said.

Every call Terry had made so far had been dead-on perfect, so who was I to suggest anything different? Still, I must confess that fly fishing a lake was something I simply did not understand, and so I went into this part of the project somewhat lukewarm. The prospect of sitting in a boat or float tube and blind-casting to a large expanse of still water somehow failed to get my juices stirring. But I was game for a try, so when we eased out onto Hidden Lake's glassy surface, I was at least curious.

"So how does this work," I asked.

"Well, we'll start out working the edges of the weedbeds and then casting to the rises," Terry patiently explained.

"The hardest part is letting your fly sit and not casting immediately to the next rise. Otherwise, they'll lead you all over the lake." He then told me how to read the trout's size, direction of travel, what food they were keying on, their family heritage and general philosophical tendencies and religious beliefs by the shape and sound of their rises and said not to worry, I'd get the hang of it.

I dutifully cast to the first rise, let the fly sit for a few seconds even though two more trout rose nearby, and there was a sudden gurgling gulp within whose rings my fly vanished. I struck on sight, or maybe it was the sound, and we were off to the rodeo.

The trout dove deep, and just as I was thinking I might have to return to shore to upsize my gear, she erupted from the surface so far out in front of us that I simply could not fathom that this was the same trout to whom I was connected. But indeed it was, and minutes later Terry slid the net beneath her and then released her as carefully as we had caught her.

By then I was an absolute basket case, eagerly searching for more rises. And they were there, one after another, each trout larger than nearly any other I had ever caught.

Now I understood exactly why Frank had insisted that Terry get me out onto these lakes, just as I also knew there would be intense inquiry and commentary at dinner this evening centering around my Tennessee trout and how they stacked up to these sub-surface buckaroos from Frank's home sweet home.

Frank Simms can be relentless.

Still, it was a valid, or perhaps not so valid, question that lingered in my own mind, not so much on Frank's behalf, but simply for myself.

How *did* these trout compare to our finicky fish back home?

Most of our wild trout in Tennessee held graduate degrees in human psychology and leader awareness, and they always seemed to be much more selective, not to mention downright suspicious, than any Western trout I had ever encountered.

It's not that I was actually trying to compare, mind you. That would be as pointless as trying to outfish someone. Fishing for trout – for *any* trout – is pure privilege, and anyone who seeks to better someone else while on trout water is missing the mark.

After all, a *Trout* is a *Trout*, regardless of its size or strain.

I have caught many *short* trout in my myriad days of fishing, but I have never, ever, caught a *small* trout, for each one is magnificent in and of itself, regardless of its physical stature. Each is God's own signature and bears firm evidence of the fact that He is still hard at work at this business of being creative.

True, these western trout were generally bigger and easier to catch than our trout back home, and the flies and tippets often seemed to be overly large and the air was thinner and clearer. But they were strong and beautiful and absolutely wild, and the setting was indeed *muy grande*.

But above all they were *Trout*, and they equally fed my spirit each time one rose to my fly, whether he actually took it or not. For the quality of the experience lay more in the encounter than in any score we could possibly have kept.

And there was still that brown trout we had to catch.

Over the next few days we fished creeks large and small, and we often returned to the high lakes as Terry and Frank showed us even more of the ranch and its resources. And there were always the trout, some so small as to fit neatly into the palm of my hand, and some so large that they would barely fit the net. But regardless of their size, they were all magnificent. There were brookies, rainbows and cutthroats enough for any fly fisherman's desires, but for some unknown reason we had yet to catch a brown trout, though Terry assured me it was simply a matter of time.

But time was now running short. So on the last morning Terry and I headed for the extreme upper reaches of the Brazos where its West and East forks converge. Just a few yards up the West Fork, Terry climbed atop a huge boulder whose leading edge formed a massive pocket in the stream below, where he spotted a sizeable form in the dark water.

I crossed the creek downstream and worked my way back up and into position to make a proper cast. As the fly drifted into its sight window, the trout rose and inhaled it.

She immediately swirled and headed for the depths, but then she unexpectedly jumped, and for a moment I thought we may have our brown, for her color was uncharacteristically golden. But the deep slash of scarlet along her sides unmistakably marked her as a rainbow. As Terry's camera clicked away above me, she jumped again, and after five more minutes I was finally able to bring her to the net.

As soon as she was revived, we crossed the hundred yards to the mouth of the East Fork, where we spent the morning fishing our way upstream, focused now on that unexpectedly elusive brown trout. But brookies and rainbows continued to dominate the program and they all performed like virtuosos, finely tuned and on their game.

As we continued to move upstream, we could see that the canyon ahead narrowed to a slot between two massive rock walls where the creek disappeared around a bend between a pair of large boulders. It was here that Terry again climbed the rocks and spotted a matched set of big rainbows quartering back and forth in a dance they had clearly performed before.

A gain I moved in below Terry and quietly crossed to the far side and began easing upstream, following his directions from above. Once in position I could clearly read the run as it swept past the upper ledge before swinging across to my left and then downstream around me.

The sun had by now moved up-canyon, showering its light across the water and giving its undulating surface a sheen like quicksilver. Even with my polarized glasses it was nearly impossible to tell what was happening beneath its rippling surface, and I waited anxiously for Terry's directions.

"*He's there!*" Terry suddenly called. "He's working the edge of the current nearest you, about eight feet below the outer point of that second big rock."

I laid the fly seven-and-a-half feet above where Terry had indicated and watched in frustration as it scooted a foot too far into the current. I let it swing far past the crease where I suspected the trout lay before carefully lifting and redepositing it back upstream, this time an inch or so outside the main flow.

As it danced back down the edge of the swift current, I gathered the spare line to me, so that when the trout finally rose and hesitated and then daintily sipped the fly, all I had to do was lift the rod and feel the hook sink deep into his upper jaw.

H is broad, powerful tail slashed in one great protesting arc that fragmented the surface glare into a million reflective shards. The trout immediately tore upstream in an instinctive attempt to gain the dark water beneath the upper ledge, and just as instinctively

I arched my rod hard over to the left in a determined attempt to deny him the position.

It worked, and in his frustration he instead chose the air, hanging there frozen in front of me nearly at eye level, the sunlight bathing every dappled inch of him before he twisted back into the creek.

His next run took him downstream and nearly past me, but I pivoted with him as he tore back upstream in one final, desperate lunge for the boulders. But his strength was waning, and now I applied every bit of pressure I could afford in order to bring him in before he was too spent. Still, once I had him securely in hand, I had to feather him back and forth in the edge of the current for a minute or more before he finally realized he was free. He left with a slash of his tail that wet down my face and glasses.

In my focused excitement, I had completely forgotten that there was a second trout. But Terry had been diligently searching the run as I worked to properly release the first fish, and he finally spotted him high up in the head of the pool.

It was impossible for me to reach him from where I was positioned, so I moved a few yards upstream and farther out into the middle of the run in order to gain a better angle. But by now Terry had lost him again, and so by mutual assent I laid my hopper close against the upper boulder, not feeling particularly good about the cast and trying to decide whether to lift the fly in mid-drift and reposition it, when Terry exclaimed, "Here he comes! Wait ... *wait* ... "

Was Terry *serious*?

The answer came in a massive swirl that seemed to take half the stream down with the fly, and as I struck I felt a weight that made the first trout seem Bush League. Upstream he turned, then dove for the bottom and ran deep beneath the upper boulder.

He settled there and sulked for nearly a minute, and frankly there wasn't a heck of a lot I could do about it except hold on and maintain a low angle of pressure to keep the tippet from abrading along the darkened underside of the ledge.

Then I felt him shake his massive head and begin to lose his grip on the current, slowly yielding to the steady pressure of the rod. From there it was pretty much a matter of patience, keeping him centered above me between the boulders, gaining every meter then every inch I could as the flow brought him slowly to me until I was finally able to slip my hand beneath him.

He was unexpectedly fresh and seemed to be more embarrassed and confused than tired. He regained his strength surprisingly fast without ever really admitting to having been caught, then tore back upstream and deep into the dark water he had just left.

The moment was as golden as the sheen on the water in which I still knelt. I looked up and around at this magnificent place, then lifted my gaze to the top of the boulder high above and returned Terry's broad grin.

For a moment, time was frozen for each of us. The accomplishment was at least as much Terry's as it was mine, for he was the maestro who had orchestrated this whole affair.

Two great rainbows, each brought to hand and cleanly released. Twenty minutes of pure exhilaration, a perfect convergence of past and future that burnished the present, indelibly etching it into memory for as long as either of us should live.

And perhaps beyond.

I recrossed the stream and climbed to where Terry was still perched on his narrow ledge, and for the first time I viewed the entire vista from his perspective. Now I could see it as clearly as he had seen it and marvel at the calls, all the perfect calls, he had made. We may even have sighted one of the two huge trout, still trying to understand what had just happened to him, and for a moment I thought I caught our own reflection in the pool far below.

And now it all seemed complete, yet another perfect end to another perfect day, our *final* day, and I could have taken down my fly rod right then, even though the afternoon was still freshening, and we could have made our way back up and over the divide and across the western slope to the lodge.

It seemed the proper thing to do, for the sky all around us suddenly and almost imperceptibly began to alter its demeanor and to murmur a low, barely audible rumble, and now even the brown trout that somehow had eluded us all these days seemed remote.

Remote perhaps, but not forgotten.

For if we left now, would we wonder in a few hours or a few days, or even in a few months or years what might have been?

Could we really leave this one thing undone?

So in the waning hours of afternoon, we crossed into the main valley of the Poso, a grand sweeping vista that had burned its image into my memory years earlier.

In summer this high valley is an elegant, green and growing place, and in autumn it is scarcely less, the surrounding ridges neatly clothed in spruce and fir and pockets of gold- and-ivory aspens all quaking with a vibrant staccato whisper in the rarefied breezes.

Only in winter does it turn a still and silent white.

Far down at the end of the valley, the redrock canyon walls really do not seem all that massive until you have trekked toward them for an hour or so and realize they still have not grown appreciably larger, and you gradually become aware of the grand scale of the space of which you are ever so briefly a part.

But now the breezes were beginning to be stirred by storms building to the north, and the sky around us was either complaining about our being here or complementing our presence, and I couldn't quite tell which it was. But the low, distant rumbling continued to echo from afar, and we could feel the thin air slowly changing as we set off down the valley in our singular search for that one missing brown trout.

At first the stream was a deceptively casual little affair as it wandered aimlessly along, gradually gaining texture and width every few hundred yards. But then it seemed to turn more deliberately down the valley through a small pristine stand of blue spruce, as though it were somehow trying to escape undetected before angling off purposefully toward the tall canyon cliffs still far below.

It was here that Terry said we would begin fishing, and the wind began to swirl and we lost ten degrees almost immediately and the air seemed suddenly to ionize.

The first trout took my tiny Royal Coachman and carried it deep beneath a grassy overhang and back into a dark pool below the spruce, then leapt and threw the Coachman back at me.

Again I cast, and again the little fly disappeared, and the next four casts produced four more trout, each stronger than the one that preceded it, each brought to hand and carefully released, each a brookie bigger than any I had ever caught.

But still no brown.

By now the tiny water droplets were beginning to gather in earnest, initially not much more than a heavy mist but quickly consolidating their forces, first into a light shower, then into a hard, wind-driven rain that sought to penetrate any weakness it could discover in my waterproof outer jacket. The once-distant rumbles now thundered as they marched full force across the pale blue ridgelines, and in awe I turned and looked skyward as the storm broke on us from all sides.

But the brown trout that took my fly drew my entire focus back to the creek.

Immediately he leapt, and I laid the rod hard over into the driving rain so my line could clear the water-laden grass overhanging the flow. But instead of diving for the bottom, he tore wildly upcurrent and crossed a little shoal into the next deep run, and I had to move with him as he dove toward the dark undercut beneath the spruce.

It was all I could do to maintain any semblance of control, not over the brown but over my own euphoria, for lightning ripped the sky and thunder filled the valley as sheets of rain filled the air.

Again the trout cleared the water by a good two feet and then broke back downstream past me. I moved to get below him and, ignoring the net, finally brought him to hand, lifting him only long enough to slip the tiny barbless hook from his upper jaw before laying him back into the churning water.

And now the thunder roared a magnum roar, as though I had robbed the high country of its one final jewel, and it mattered not that I had only photographed him, for lightning again rent the sky from seam to seam, in its rage tearing open her bare underbelly and letting forth all the storm it could muster.

I do so love a storm; but only then did I realize that I had put Terry in an impossible position, for I had been too stubborn and selfish in my own pursuit of this one final brown trout, ignoring the fact that it was *Terry* who was responsible not only for showing me these places, but also for keeping me from doing something stupid and getting hurt.

The high country is absolutely no place to be careless with storms such as these, which can build for days before unleashing themselves in one massive, elegant gesture. Terry was hunkered down in his raincoat at the base of a little rise far across the valley, and at a signal we both turned and made for the safety of the truck, my last few hundred yards a telling reminder of the elevation and the final fulfilling release into the reality of what had been up until now mere hope.

And still I lingered, fully a part of the storm, that wonderful signature storm, savoring the experience and trying to make it last for just one moment more.

We had finally done what we'd come here to do, and for the first time I actually felt the altitude as I hurried back up the broad slope, my breath coming labored as I pushed head-on into the driving storm, feeding impressions into my little digital pocket recorder.

But no matter. My breath would soon return, for it was now my *own* spirit who roared, a spirit kindred to the thunder that seemed to come at me from all directions, a spirit that roared with exhilaration, not in any singular achievement but merely in the experience; a spirit who roared with the privilege of having encountered God face to face in His own element and of hearing His voice in the thunder and feeling His breath in the wind and His tears in the water streaming down my face, as though He were marking His approval of the moment and indelibly signing off on it.

It was done.

I and the fishing were complete, as complete as anything I have ever known. I was overwhelmed with the perfection of what had just occurred, and as if on cue God roared again and ripped the sky in one final expression of divine approbation.

From that first big brookie days earlier below Carly's boulder to the gilded rainbow I had sworn was a brown trout when she first leapt; from those massive rainbows in the diminutive lakes to the bejeweled Rio Grande cutthroats that had stopped me in my tracks, and clear up to this one final brown, my storm trout Gift on this storm perfect day, it would take a long, long time to dissect and digest it all and fully comprehend what had just happened.

I'm still working on it.

CHAPTER 19

A COVE CREEK
FRAGMENT

"There was another fisherman,
one who obviously knew how to catch
and properly land a trout . . ."

I f my first trout is merely an imagined dream, then the first trout I actually remember is still as fresh as it was when the leader finally broke and the fish fell out of my small world and back into its own. You'd think it would have been Dad who was there with me, but he was busy dumping coal from the tipple that sat across the hollow from the mine, loading its contents into giant railroad cars and filling the air with coal dust that coated him and all around him with a fine blackness until only his eyes were white.

That was our world back then: black and white, white and black, with not much more than grey to buffer the reality of keeping small children warm and families fed. So while Dad dumped coal, Mom and I and Bobby and Aunt Ruth headed across Stoney Ridge to Cove Creek for a day of provision and sport.

I was only five years old, and I don't remember getting there, but it surely must have been in Uncle Sylvie's blue, two-tone Buick, because we didn't have a car of our own back then. Uncle Sylvie wasn't with us either, though he and I fully intended to go trout fishing just as soon as we could. But for now he was deep in the mine, loading coal and sending it out to the tipple where Dad would then grade it and dump it into the long black trains.

I don't remember getting to the creek that day or carrying our gear through the woods and down the wooded trail to the water. And I don't remember how Mom and I managed to climb out onto the big rock that sat four feet above the current.

But I *do* remember that it was only wide enough for one mother, one five-year-old, our fishing rod and bait and our dinner. And I remember how excited she was when she finally hooked her trout and how it hung there below us while she tried to decide how best to land it, and how carefully she worked the trout up to us, trying not to break the line or get it tangled in the thick brush that edged the creek bank.

And I *certainly* remember how rough and abrasive the weathered rock felt through my tee shirt and on my bare arms as I lay there facing the trout, reaching, reaching, reaching for the line until I finally had it firmly in my chubby little hands, and how the monofilament leader nearly cut me as I lifted it, trout and all, from the water. The fish and I watched each other eye to eye as it twisted and cavorted against the roughened stone, rising until it was nearly within my grasp. But the thinning leader finally reached its abrasion limit and parted, and it took the trout a long time to fall back into the stream.

I don't think Mom had ever before caught a trout, and it was not for herself that she wanted to catch it. It was for Dad, for his grin, for his pleasure and his approval and for how proud he would have been for her. Not *of* her, but *for* her; he was already proud *of* her and could be no prouder, for that's the way they always were.

Her disappointment, however, was total and deep, and she ran from the rock back to the car to get another hook, declaring to all the world that if anyone else caught that trout, it was hers.

And you know, that's exactly what happened.

You see, there was another fisherman, one who obviously knew how to properly hook and land a trout, one who showed up an hour before dark, the most perfect hour for trout, and began fishing not very far downstream from the big rock that was still draped in disappointment when most everyone else had gone home.

He fished the creek the way it should be fished, hard and with great efficiency and precision, moving smoothly upstream from rock to pool to run to rock like a dancer.

He fished deliberately and wasted no effort as he probed the likely spots for the fish he instinctively knew must be there. For he, too, had a family who regularly fed on trout.

He came in from below, carefully and methodically fishing each run as he made his way upstream, his final focus the swirling eddy below the big rock where he knew the trout would likely be working their evening feeding lanes.

He already had four fish before he reached the run below our rock, for fishermen such as this know how to catch trout. But he certainly had room for one more in his old canvas creel as he stepped into position at the tail end of the eddy and began casting.

His drifts were surgical and precise, and when the trout struck, he set the hook neither too softly nor too hard. And whether he noticed the frayed leader hanging from the trout's mouth as he carefully worked it to his net, I have no way of knowing.

But he *did* see it when he lifted the fish from the stream and slipped his own hook from the corner of its jaw, deliberately leaving the other hook with its trailing tippet firmly in place so he could show it to Mom and me when he finally got home that night.

- CHAPTER 20 -

PRAYERS OF THE RIVER

"They flowed around me
barely three feet off the water,
and for a few mystical moments I found
I was actually in the midst of their formation."

Sometimes I go to the river to pray, and sometimes the prayers simply grow of their own accord, spawned by care and question and need that the fishing and the river set free and allow to surface, up from the dark depths of worry and the world in which I spend the larger portion of my life.

These prayers are born in an instant, then flow unbound both outward and inward into an unfathomable stillness of peace and receptivity, where they are gathered by Him to whom they are sent to be caressed and considered and then returned with an infinite peace to their source to sooth and clarify the soul that first gave them wing.

There are other ways I could go, but I prefer to go by the river.

As I drove along beside it this morning on my way in to the studio, the river had overrun its banks and the quiet morning fog was playing among the trees and meadows, indulging itself in a world it only occasionally visits.

My hand hung loosely out the window of the car, feathering the cool morning air, and the mist flowed through my fingers as perhaps it had flowed, while it was still water, along the sides of the big brown trout I had released far upstream late last evening.

He'd been badly hooked in the face just behind his left eye, and I had slipped him alone into my flow-through creel and hung him from my wading belt in the river facing upstream to comfort him and keep him cool. He was still very much alive and complaining thirty minutes later, and so I gently and tentatively placed him back into the eddy of my waders and watched as he reoriented himself to the river and finally eased from my hands.

If his face was torn, his color and demeanor were still strong and good. And this morning I wondered if the mist that now comforted me had somehow comforted him during the night while it was still water.

There is always comfort in the water. It is a separate reality not associated with the world through which I must pass in order to occasionally become one with it. When I step through the river's surface and find myself surrounded by her in every direction, I temporarily become a small part of the entire ecosystem, along with the trout and the ducks and the geese, the otter and beaver and muskrats.

I have watched them all since late last winter – that first pair of Canada geese prospecting their nest site at the head of the island; the mallards whistling through the wind as I etched the air with my fly line; the otter rising like an apparition from the twilight face of the water to try and figure out what I was.

There was the lone hen mallard with the seven mottled chicks that the following week were five and are now down to three, but three nearly full-grown Susies that hopefully next year will find responsible mates and have broods of their own.

By contrast, there was the mated pair of wild mallards that when I first saw them had five chicks, and when I saw them yesterday evening still had all five, firmly attesting to the importance of active fatherhood.

The best I can tell, there have been either six or seven families of Canada geese along the stretch of river that contains the Otter Pool, and I have watched them all since that first prospecting pair I spotted last winter at the head of the island. There is nothing finer than seeing a father goose cautiously and proudly leading his family on a warm summer morning as they glide upstream through the rising mist, the goslings lined up in his wake with their mother acting as rear guard, then watching them grow as they and the seasons inevitably age.

Yesterday morning I watched as all six or seven families came flying upriver through the late-summer air around me, and I could not tell the parents from their young. They had neither fear nor regard for me as I ceased casting and lowered my rod as they approached at eye level.

They flowed around me barely four feet off the water, and for a few mystical moments I found I was actually in the midst of their formation. I could sense the vortices emanating from their pulsing wing-tips, and if I could have joined them I would have flown in these pockets of lesser turbulence and become a part of their vee.

I have not seen the otter in months, but yesterday morning a young beaver entered the water from behind me and was partway across the river before I noticed his wake from the corner of my eye as I changed flies. He swam all the way across the current and then eased out of the water to climb a grassy ramp on the far side where he disappeared into a tangle of wood that until then I had thought was only random and had not recognized as a beaver lodge.

A kingfisher rocketed upriver on his way to breakfast, chattering loudly and declaring his presence to all the world.

But except for that one fish that I hooked in the face, the trout more or less left me alone, as though they knew there were more important things for me to do than catch them. I could see them occasionally flashing deep in the belly of the run, and at first I thought they were bottom-feeding. But the water was not as cool as usual and the sun was close with its Dog Days demeanor, robbing the river of its rain and the sky its clouds and making the water unusually warm and most likely uncomfortable for the trout.

And so I tucked my fly into its keeper loop at the base of the rod and slowly eased back downstream, through the Otter Pool, past the head of the island, then across and out of the river and up the trail to my car and home, leaving my prayers floating Heavenward with the evening.

– Chapter 21 –

 Codgers and
Coots

"In its ultimate form,
a true Codger isn't even fully aware
of his own Codgerism."

don't know who they are or why they're there, but I just saw them again upriver near the Otter Pool as I drove out, still in my waders. They're just sitting there, two old guys in their '72 Chevy . . . you know, the big one with the body that's square on both ends and seems too large for its tires.

One of them probably swapped his '55 for it back in the early '80s, and he likely didn't get more than two or three hundred dollars trade-in. But considering that's probably about half of what he paid for it originally, I guess it wasn't too bad a deal.

Anyhow, they were still sitting up there a few minutes ago.

They're always there on Sunday afternoon. And Wednesday and Friday for all I know. They just sit parked by the river, and I don't think I've ever seen them actually talking to each other.

They just sit there, *being*. I unintentionally made eye contact with the driver as I passed them a few minutes ago and felt obliged to toss him a wave. He didn't seem to mind and even lifted a palm in greeting back at me.

don't know if they are Codgers or Coots. I suppose that would depend entirely on who you asked. But for my part, I would like to think they are *Codgers*. A Codger has already done just about anything worth doing, at least in his own mind, and so he really doesn't much give a flip or anything else about what others may think; at least that's what he'll tell you *and* himself if confronted by either.

He might simply be an "Old Codger," or in its more honorable form a "Smart Ol' Codger." But in the end the operative word is "Codger" and the degree doesn't much matter.

On the other hand, if you consult their wives, they will most likely refer to them as "Coots." The actual degree of Cootism is irrelevant, because to their wives, all Coots are totally and completely worthless. This may even be ratified with such terms as "Worthless Old Coot" or "Crazy Old Coot" or some other descriptor equally or even more derisive. But in the end it all comes down to "Coot."

I cannot imagine anyone intentionally setting out to be a Coot.

C odgerism, on the other hand, is a worthwhile endeavor. You can't learn to be a Codger; it is an acquired state. I would think you must be at least sixty years of age to qualify as a Codger, in spirit if not in body.

Being a Codger has little to do with accomplishment or wealth, although the higher the worldly status a man attains, the more difficult it may be to remain a true Codger.

These guys may be dirt poor, or they may be gajillionaires, one of the group of locals who have a Valley or a Ridge or even a Development named after their family if not themselves, most likely derived from lands that were bought for pennies an acre when the '55 was still a pipe dream, and who later sold that same land for a bloody fortune.

A man like this is considered to be a Codger among Codgers, at least by fellow Codgers, for they refuse to let the standards of the world interfere with their Codgeristic inclinations.

In its ultimate manifestation, a true Codger probably isn't even fully aware of his own Codgerism.

A Coot, on the other hand, is *completely* aware of his status. His wife or some other self-worthy female will surely see to that. It's her duty, you see, her primary purpose in life. That's why she's down here on earth, and that's why they're up there by the river at this very moment, trying their best to be Codgers, if for no other reason than to simply get away for a little while.

You know, now that I think about it, I don't suppose those guys *are* parked up by the Otter Pool on Wednesday or Friday, or any other day of the work week for that matter. Otherwise they would not have felt compelled to go up there this afternoon.

But then again, neither would I.

Which raises the somewhat sobering question in my own mind: Does this make me a Codger-in-Training?

Or perhaps simply a fledgling Coot?

CHAPTER 22

ALASKA:
FLY FISHING
THE LAST GREAT LAND

"I would never have presumed
to venture into the last great land.
That's what 'Alaska' means, you know,
"The Great Land."

For the first time in my life, I was leaving Alaska. I had never before *left* Alaska, for until now Alaska was a place I had never been. So with the backpack strung over my shoulder, I took one last look around inside my empty tent, then stepped outside and into the path Leota and I had walked together daily and headed down the trail to the gravel bar and the boat where Matthew Hynes was waiting for me as he had waited so many mornings.

The bulk of my gear – my fly rods and waders and large duffel – had left on another boat an hour earlier headed downriver to Quinhagak and would be waiting for me beside the little gravel airstrip just outside the village on the coast of the Bering Sea.

I nearly walked straight into the Kanektok as I approached the small boat, momentarily forgetting that I was wearing my old flying boots instead of my waders. I would not take these boots off for the next day and a half, not until I touched down back home in the mountains of East Tennessee where Mary Jane and Carly would be waiting to meet me.

But for now I had other mountains to cross: the Ahklun and the Kilbuck that formed the looming horizon eighty miles to the east, then the Alaska Range and the Chugash and the entire expanse of the Canadian and American Rockies before crossing out over the plains and into my native Appalachians.

But first, I had to make it into the boat without getting my feet wet.

The run down to the sea and the Yupik village of Quinhagak along the coast was now comfortably familiar, and I instinctively leaned into every bend as Matt threaded the skiff past the beaver lodge and the grizzly beach and the Yupik day camp and the *Zoo Bar,* where I had caught the giant chinook, and I mentally marked every salmon, trout and Dolly Varden I could remember along the way.

Matt eased back on the throttle as we rounded the last bend above the village, and as he nosed the boat onto the gravel bar, I stepped lightly out onto shore. He handed me my backpack and we firmly shook hands and said an awkward goodbye, made so by the deep friendship we had formed while fishing together. And as the sound of his motor gradually faded upriver, leaving me to savor this one last silence, I found myself again alone in Alaska.

I momentarily paused and for the final time looked up into the low-hanging sky, listening to the quiet whisper of the river and the rustling of the wind through the willows and then the soft crunch of the ancient gravel beneath my feet as I headed up the trail to the truck that would carry me through the village and out to the airstrip.

Alaska had been the idea of my long-time friend and publisher Chuck Wechsler, not my own. I would never have presumed to venture into the last great land – that's what "Alaska" means, you know, *"The Great Land."*

Alaska had always been a compelling place for me, abstract and mysterious both in its meaning and in its ability to gather together all the boundaries I had ever known and then ball them up into one small and insignificant bundle and shred them before my very eyes.

"You've never fished *Alaska*?" Chuck asked.

"No sir, I haven't."

It would have never occurred to me to fish Alaska. Alaska was simply too far removed, not just geographically, but experientially as well. Alaska had always seemed to be something you had to grow into. And though I had fished for longer than I could remember, my most distant trips afield with a fly rod had been to New Mexico and the Great Lakes and northern Ontario, and my only really large fish had been the salmon and steelhead from the tributaries of Michigan and Huron, and of course the saltwater inhabitants along the Outer Banks. I simply wasn't ready for Alaska, and I wasn't at all certain Alaska would be ready for me.

But *this*, I finally realized, was precisely why I had to go.

For I sensed that Alaska must be so vast, both in miles and in spirit, that anyone who has never been there and still thinks they are ready for her is either arrogant or ignorant, and at given times in my life I have surely been both.

My initial inclinations were to learn as much about Alaska as I could before I actually went there. But somewhere, sometime during the process, it became clear that I should instead allow Alaska *herself* to be the teacher once I met her soul to soul, rather than trying to learn her for myself from afar. So the patience of years trumped the exuberance of youth, and I was content to wait and meet her in person, not at all certain whether she would turn out to be a friend, a lover, or merely a distant, one-time acquaintance.

Chuck called in late June with arrangements for me to fish with Alaska West, a long-standing icon of Alaskan fly fishing. The problem was that the peak of the salmon runs was just a couple of weeks away, and if I were to make it on time I would have to be on a plane in a matter of days. Chuck and Alaska West owner Andrew Bennett feared – and I reluctantly confirmed – that there was simply too little time for me to arrange and rearrange schedules, get all my gear in order, and pull everything together.

We all agreed that the best thing to do was for me to recycle until the following July and experience Alaska at her fullest, for it is in mid-summer that the Pacific salmon are home from the sea and the opportunities to catch all five species are at their peak.

First are the *chinook*, or king, salmon, the legendary giants of the species. Then there are the *chum*, nearly as grand as the kings and much more prolific. The *sockeye* and the *pink* salmon, though somewhat smaller, are also present in great numbers. Finally, the *silver*, or coho, salmon are the last to run and therefore would be the most likely to shut us out if we were not in the right place at the right time.

But even more attractive for me were the legendary leopard rainbows that inhabit these waters, along with good numbers of Dolly Varden and a smattering of grayling. The Dolly Varden is not actually a trout but a char, like our native brookies back home, and the grayling is the epitome of the north country, unable to live in lesser climes and therefore potentially the essence of the entire experience.

I kept my hopes for grayling more or less to myself, sharing them only with my brothers and sister and, of course, Chuck; I knew they were relatively rare where I was going and my chances of connecting with them would be much slimmer than with the salmon and trout.

Catching a grayling was, in fact, one of the few preconceptions that I allowed myself during the year leading up to departure, a time in which to discover for myself how I should think about Alaska and about where it was I was actually going.

The anticipation continued to build as months dissolved into weeks and weeks into days until the hour finally came to board the plane in Tennessee, where I hugged Mary Jane and Carly before going through security, then paused as I hauled my pack up onto my shoulder and looked back at them one last time and left all I had ever known behind.

And now I fast-forward, first south along the broad spine of the Appalachians and into Atlanta, then north and west out over the Great Plains and the Rockies, across into Canada and up the Pacific coast of British Columbia, then high above the Chugash mountains into Anchorage, where I stopped and slept for a few hours.

The next morning it was west across the entire expanse of the Alaska Range to Bethel, where the small bush plane picked me up and carried me south, low across the water-pocked tundra to the little gravel landing strip at Quinhagak, a thriving Yupik Indian village on the coast of the Bering Sea.

Eighty miles east I could see the intersecting ranges of the Ahklun and Kilbuck mountains where the Kanektok River springs from its mother lake, *Kagati*. But by now the sensory and intellectual overload was simply overwhelming, and as we motored upriver I found myself completely incapable of comprehending that there were likely no other humans along my line of sight east to the mountains.

Forty-five minutes later, Matthew angled us into the little side channel below camp where soon-to-be friends were waiting to shepherd me and my gear to my tent and to dinner and then finally out into the Last Great Land.

CHAPTER 23

THE RIVER OF
MANY CHANGES

"Trout, fly, and a sizeable chunk of the river
erupted into the crisp morning air . . ."

The fresh grizzly tracks that skirted the coarse, sandy shoreline were still moist and crumbling as we eased the crippled boat through the morning fog and up onto the narrow beach. As I quietly stepped out and began intently examining the bear tracks, Matthew Hynes was just as intently examining the outboard motor and finally whispered, "I'm not exactly sure what's going on here. It looks like one of the mounting pins has broken."

With my own mechanical skills lagging considerably behind Matt's, our only solution was to hike a mile back upriver, cross the broad flow to camp and bring down another boat.

As for me, we both agreed I would be of much greater benefit to the whole mission, not to mention much less an encumbrance to Matt, if I were simply to stay here alone, to fish among the unseen grizzlies and photograph their ubiquitous tracks. So as my trusty Alaskan guide disappeared upriver into the willows, I slipped my six-weight from the boat's rod clips, slung the camera strap over my shoulder and followed the bear tracks upstream to the head of the run.

As I tied on a combination egg and flesh pattern and began casting, I could not help looking up occasionally to check for our oversized friends who had so recently left their broad, imposing signatures in the sand at my feet.

On my third drift, the fly was abruptly halted by a pulsing beat that echoed up the line and down through the rod into my hands. As I struck, the line cut an arching gash through the dappled surface, and the fish burrowed deep and behaved rudely as I circled to get below it. Four minutes later, I managed to slip the wooden net beneath her, a long lightly-hued Dolly Varden perfectly fit for a memory.

I photographed her quickly in the net alongside the grizzly tracks, then patiently revived and released her and moved back up the narrow beach to the head of the run. Again I cast, the line rolling effortlessly through the cool morning air and easing the little fly into the upper edge of the current, and again some spirit unseen hammered the tiny offering near the end of the drift. With emotions beginning to overflow, I lifted my face to the sky and smiled at God's impeccable sense of timing and the improbable setting in which He had placed me, here alone with the grizzlies and the fish in the vast Alaska wilderness with the river and the wind whispering quietly to me through the mist.

Never had I felt more in tune with the Infinite.

For her part, this Dolly obviously had plans of her own, none of which seemed to include me. But minutes later, just as we were finally beginning to come to a loose understanding, I heard the low rumble of a fresh motor easing downriver and looked up to see Matt standing and giving directions, with our friend Chris Price at the controls.

They arrived just as I was reaching for the tethered net on my wading belt. As Matt went to work with the camera, Chris quickly identified and remedied the issues with the motor mount, and moments later with the Dolly Varden and me both released and the mist beginning to lift, Matt and I were again weaving our way up this broad and most-aptly named river in our continuing quest for enlightenment.

It is called the "Kanektok," and in the native Alaskan Yupik language it means "The River of Many Changes." We had just begun our last day together on this compelling river, Matthew and I, completely absorbed in a fly-fishing adventure that had been conceived more than a year earlier. Now as we eased upstream through the cool morning air I had no way of knowing that, aside from any day I ever spent fishing with my Dad, the finest day's fishing I have ever experienced had just begun here along its ever-changing shoreline.

The Kanektok is a broad, braided river, its sinuous strands interwoven through the trees and the tundra, its bed a moveable mix of multi-colored stones and glacial spew.

It is famous for its prolific runs of all five species of Pacific salmon, as well as for its legendary leopard rainbows. Add to this a compelling mix of Dolly Varden and even a chance at grayling, and you have some of the finest fly-fishing opportunities in the world.

We had begun our adventures a week earlier, for the first few days focusing our attention primarily on the salmon. You can do nothing but respect and admire these great and noble fish, who after years at sea have returned home to the rivers of their birth, not simply to spawn and die, but to pass their bodies and spirits along to others.

Over three-quarters of the fertilizing nitrogen in these river systems comes either directly or indirectly from the annual salmon runs, with roughly 125 individual species of plants, animals, fish and even insect life dependent upon them for their own survival.

On the first evening in camp, after stowing my gear and assembling my fly rods, Matt and I had headed down the Kanektok by boat. We anchored along a narrowing funnel he called the *Zoo Bar*, and I began swinging a large chartreuse fly along a sweeping arch from the outer edge of the wooded shore to the shallows that lay downstream. We only had a couple of hours left before dinner, so this was actually intended to be just a shakedown run in preparation for the days ahead.

But one particularly large chinook salmon had other intentions.

He struck on a downstream mend with an attitude that seemed to convey his resentment of this northern intrusion by a southern boy like me, as though he meant to kick me around and show me for real what a fish from Alaska was all about.

I thought I was pretty good at this sort of thing, having caught chinook up to thirty pounds in some of the Great Lakes tributaries; but this fish was a home boy on his own turf, and before I could completely process what was happening, I was watching my backing chase my rapidly disappearing fly line downstream into the face of the west wind raging upriver from the Bering Sea.

Still, my reel was up to the challenge and the great fish was eventually compelled to reconsider his exit strategy, and twelve minutes later we had him within thirty feet of the boat. Thinking the situation was now pretty much in hand, I must confess I was surprised when the blood-red king cautiously surfaced, cast an indignant glance up in our direction and decided to leave again.

If his first panicked run had been a study in power, his second was a thing of absolute beauty and control. Again my fly line flew from the sweetly singing Tibor, and again I prayed the connection to the backing was up to the challenge.

But the vintage cork drag was still smooth and cool and reassuring, and another ten minutes saw the big chinook nearing the boat once more, this time with a quizzical look on his gnarled face as he surfaced twenty-five yards behind us to reassess his position.

His third run was not quite so dramatic as the first two, this time ripping barely fifty yards of backing from the reel.

"We'd best head for shore and try to beach him there," Matt declared.

As he rowed toward the bar, I loosened the drag ever so slightly and eased off on the rod pressure in an attempt to bring us to a temporary standstill until I could step out onto the gravel where the fish and I could commence final negotiations.

Once on shore, I scrambled to get below him, applying opposing angles of pressure and lower, more powerful rod positions, and another ten minutes saw him nearly to the beach, where Matt was finally able to get the net beneath him.

He was magnificent, a deep coral red from stem to stern, his face, jaws, back and underbelly splotched with rich tones of amber and olive and bronze. His huge toothy jaw pulsed in the shallow water and his broad body undulated as though he were still contending for his life and the lives of his progeny-to-be.

But he would not die here – not today, not by *my* hand – for I lifted him from the river only long enough for Matthew to photograph him, then took all the time each of us needed to regain our strength and composure before returning to our respective lives' work.

Personally, I called it a draw, for I was at least as spent as the great fish, and it was Matt who had finally and mercifully called it a day and declared it was time for us to head back upriver to camp and supper.

The following days had been some of the finest of my fly-fishing life, interwoven with the river and the salmon and the privilege of experiencing Alaska for the first time. In addition to more kings, we caught chum salmon, their signature marled sides striking and dramatic, whether they were in the water or in the air. We caught pinks, the males with their distinctive humps, and the hens silver-sided and still virtuous.

We even caught a magnificent male sockeye when we swung a large streamer a little too close to his *redd*, or nest, in a discreet little side channel where they had gathered by the dozens. He was characteristically crimson and hook-jawed, with his electric green head aglow. We chose, however, to not further disturb these sockeye while they were on their beds and so left them alone to complete their work in private.

We had been a few days too early for this year's primary runs of silvers, but we barely considered it a loss, for we couldn't possibly have been any happier. And finally after so many days spent fighting the heavyweights, we determined it was time to focus on the rainbows, Dolly Varden and *dare we hope*, for grayling.

So now on this, our final day together, and with the motor once more fully functional, we left the Dolly Varden and grizzlies behind and headed upriver into the low morning light.

The lower Kanektok is wide and mature as it nears its rendezvous with the Bering Sea, its sweeping bends broad and patient, as though it knows its long journey from the mountains to the ocean will soon be complete. But the upper river where we were now headed is more lithe, like a young colt out for a run through the forest, nimble and chiseled, darting left, darting right, uncertain of its next move until it has already made it, leaping from bend to bend and shoal to shoal in its youthful impatience to reach the sea.

But we *too* were impatient as we ran upriver with our faces into the wind and the wakening day, the rising mists fleeing from the morning like the gulls along the gravel bars each time we rounded a new bend. No other place I had ever fished could have prepared me for this great river, with its eagles embracing the sky above us on broad, powerful wings, and its bears and caribou lurking unseen but certain in the low forests and tall grasses that lined every trail.

But we were not out for eagles or bears or caribou this morning, but for *rainbows*, some of the most special rainbows in the world.

The Leopard Rainbows of the Kanektok are legendary for their size, their spirit, their rich coloration, and especially for their deep ebony spots, which appear even on their eyes. First and foremost these trout are opportunistic feeders, heavily dependent on the annual salmon runs for their well-being.

But if the rainbows of the Kanektok consider the eggs and flesh of salmon a dietary staple, they consider a mouse that has accidentally fallen into the river an absolute *delicacy*.

169

To that end, Matt had developed what is without doubt the finest mouse pattern I have ever seen, and we were determined to put it to the test at our earliest opportunity.

So at 8:55 on our final run upstream and with the morning sky as clear as the cold water racing beneath our boat, we pulled into the gravel shore seventy-five yards above the mouth of a narrow side channel where a small group of chinook were engrossed in their spawning.

Rainbows are notorious for setting up shop downstream from spawning salmon and picking off eggs that may drift into their sight windows. But as perfect a set-up for dead-drifting an egg pattern as this was, we simply couldn't resist the opportunity to put Matt's mouse pattern into play. I tied the fly onto a brand new piece of 5X tippet with a perfection loop and began quartering it cross-current, moving a step or two down the shoreline with each cast.

Once, we thought we detected a tentative strike about halfway through a drift. But that was all until I got nearly to the end of the run where suddenly there was a bulging swirl, then another a foot or so behind the fly. Matt had cautioned me that it would take nerves of steel to resist the urge to strike on such a massive swirl unless I actually *felt* the trout. Heeding his warning, I continued to let the mouse wake evenly downstream across the flow.

Again the trout swung at it, this time knocking it sideways into the slower water on the inside of the run. But still I fought the nearly overwhelming compulsion to strike, and so let the fly continue to track across the surface. Thinking he now had the mouse sufficiently stunned, the trout curled on it one last time, taking it completely under, and only then did I strike.

Trout, fly, line and a sizeable chunk of the river erupted into the clear morning air, the bright, backlit spray of silver and coral pink sending my heart soaring. Matt's impromptu cry of approval made the moment complete.

Positioned on the inside of the run, I immediately applied right-hand pressure to the giant trout in an effort to move him out of the strong current and into the calmer water of the nearby side channel. For a moment he burrowed deep for the bottom, then once more came three feet out of the water, this time with Matt's mouse fly showing clearly in the corner of his jaw.

Now he turned left, making for the stronger water in the middle of the river. I countered to the right and was finally able to shift him into the mouth of the side channel where Matt was waiting with the release net.

He was perhaps the most striking rainbow I had ever seen, with deep coral stripes centering his broad quicksilver sides, and his multi-hued gill plates glowing iridescent in the cool morning light. Ebony dapples covered every lovely inch from the tip of his nose to the tip of his tail and even over his eyes. His clean, nearly transparent fins were edged in ivory and absolutely pristine, and the depth of his color was exceeded only by the breadth of his spirit. He was truly one of God's originals.

We photographed him quickly and revived him slowly and last saw him as he was backing down the edge of the run and out into the main current with his noble spirit undiminished and his education on mice elevated to post-graduate level.

And now, finally, we turned our attention to grayling.

Biologically speaking, grayling belong to the whitefish family and are not salmonoids at all. But in spirit they might as well be, for with their shy nature, subtle coloration and the tall, broad dorsal fins of the males, they represent the true spirit of the north.

More than any other fish in the world, I had always wanted to catch a grayling, ever since the days of my childhood. I had read about grayling. I had seen pictures of grayling. I had watched movies and videos of grayling. Heck, I had even *been* to Grayling. But never, except in my wildest dreams of youth, did I ever imagine I might someday have the opportunity to fish for them. And now here we were, searching the flat water and the side channels for the telltale surface dapples that might betray their presence.

Matt had cautioned me that catching a grayling could be a long shot. So now as we searched for the enchanted fish, I dared not let my hopes get too high, for even if we failed to find them, I had already been blessed with some of the finest fly fishing I had ever experienced.

As late morning turned into early afternoon, we continued to explore the myriad side channels, taking one giant rainbow after another on the mouse, and even returning to the main channel whenever we would spot spawning salmon, drifting flies and mouse patterns downstream behind them where more rainbows came to our net and cameras.

Matthew was an absolute master at this business of being a guide, part technician, part psychologist, part biologist and always philosopher, artist and coach. But above all, he was my teacher and my friend, and I sensed it had become just as important to him to find a grayling as it was to me.

But the day was now beginning to ebb, and as Matt eased the boat out onto the final bar of our final day together, as far upriver as we had ventured thus far, it seemed to me that I had finally worn him down. For instead of coming with me as I began to fish the broad shelf that bisected the river, he uncharacteristically remained seated in the boat, his focus across and slightly downriver.

Little did I know.

We had caught rainbows before below these gravel shelves, which are regularly occurring structures along the Kanektok, formed by the loose, colorful stones from the geologically young mountains eighty miles to the east. The technique was to cast the fly, usually a smolt or flesh pattern, a few feet above the drop-off and let it drift over the lip of the shelf into the deep water below, then work it downstream before slowly stripping it back.

This I continued to do as I methodically worked my way along the ledge, occasionally glancing back at Matt, still seated in the boat and gazing across the river at some slack water along the far shoreline.

When the fish hit, he felt like a good one, and Matt was already on his feet and heading toward me with the net as I called *"Hooked up!"* But somehow this fish wasn't behaving quite like the other rainbows with whom we had connected, and for a moment I thought we might have a small sockeye. Then I saw it, a dark, bluish-gray, somewhat linear form with . . . *could it be?* . . . a sail!

"It's a Grayling!" I shouted, suddenly on the very edge of self-control.

I checked the drag on my reel, but it was set properly and I resisted the temptation to adjust it. But, oh, how I wanted this fish. How I had dreamed of this fish. How carefully I played this fish, and how carefully Matt finally slipped the net beneath it, and how nearly I wept as the dream of childhood became a grown man's reality.

For his part, Matt had known all along that we were in grayling water, now confessing to having spotted their subtle rises a week earlier in the flat stretch on the far side of the river he had been watching so intently from the boat as I fished. But even *he* did not expect one so huge to be hanging with the big boys beneath this ledge.

We took extreme care as we slipped the barbless hook from his jaw and quickly photographed him, then slowly revived him before easing him back into the river. He was huge, the biggest grayling Matt had ever seen, and when we measured him later that night in the digital photos alongside the six-weight, everyone determined he would go at least twenty inches.

Ironically, I was the only person in camp for whom the size did not matter; I would have settled for one much smaller. What did matter was that he was a grayling. *A grayling!* A beautiful, tall-finned, multi-hued grayling, the very essence of the north country.

Threadbare the adventure was now complete. It had begun in the wind and rain on a thirty-degree afternoon with the forty-pound chinook, then ripened through day after day of big salmon, giant rainbows, elegant Dolly Varden, and the constant closeness of bears and eagles and new friends and an ever-growing reversion to the distant days of youth. And now it was coming to an end in late-day sunshine twenty miles upriver with this marvelous and mysterious fish of a lifetime.

How was it that God had brought us together here in the final hour of our final day, this day of such absolute perfection when for the briefest moment I found myself living wholly in the present instead of looking to the past or longing for the future?

The River of Many Changes had certainly lived up to her name.

For never again would I ever be the same.

CHAPTER 24

THE TENT
(MOBIUS STRIP)

"Sometimes my line flew smoothly out over the surface,
its tight looping thrust remaining intact as it delivered the
fly perfectly to the exact point I had targeted.
But sometimes the wind would discover my treachery . . ."

In the mornings I would awaken in my tent, surrounded by the warm glow of Alaska softly seeping in through its ivory walls, then get dressed and gather my meager gear for the day ahead, slip into waders and make my way with Leota down the trail through the willows and cottonwoods to breakfast and the boat. We would spend the day on the river with the salmon and the trout and the eagles and the great Alaskan bears. In the evenings I would return to my tent.

It was a warm and soothing tent, its walls the color of thinly shaved mastodon ivory, formed on a conestoga frame with a clean wooden floor, a simple door on one end and a small translucent window on the other.

There were two single beds. One I used for sleeping and one for organizing and staging my clothes and my gear. There were two small tables, one at the head of each bed, and on these tables I kept my extra leaders, fly boxes and cameras, along with my water bottles, shaving gear and books.

The beds rested on wooden frames set on upturned galvanized buckets at the corners. My thick foam mattress was quite comfortable, covered with soft flannel sheets and light, layered quilts and blankets of cotton and wool.

My bed was enclosed with a full-coverage mosquito net, which I would pull down around me at night with great diligence, and when I returned from the Kanektok each evening, Shasta would have made my bed and stashed the netting overhead, loosely wrapping it across its own suspending cords.

It was a lovely place to have waiting for you at the end of a long day upriver or down, discreetly tucked into the trees and brush where it was sheltered from the wind and the glare of the water, and it was quiet except for the muted hum of the ever-present mosquitoes, which I took great care to keep outside my door.

Shasta's little brown and ivory spaniel, Leota, was always happy to see me when I returned from the river, and she would accompany me up the trail to my tent and drop her tennis ball at the same place each evening. I would toss it off into the bush where she would quickly find it and be back at my side by the time I reached my door, much to the delight of us both. *Leota* is a name from the Blackfoot language and means "Prairie Flower." Shasta had named her beloved little dog after her grandmother.

Once at my tent, I would stand my fly rods against its outer wall to dry, retrieving them after supper and breaking them down and bringing them inside to clean and prepare for the next day's work. I'd remove my fingerless gloves only when I had stepped safely inside, away from the mosquitoes. The mosquitoes were one of the constants, like the willows and the wind and the whisper of the river and, of course, the light.

he Light. It would begin to return from its brief absence around 4:30 each morning and would not start to fade until an hour or so after midnight. And even then it was never completely dark, even on a moonless night, and often I would pull my black stocking cap over my eyes in order to sleep. It was as integral a part of my cocoon as my netting and blankets and sleeping gloves.

It was a warm and secure place, my tent, not only for my body but for my spirit as well, and even when the temperature dipped into the thirties outside and the wind-driven rain drummed on its outer surface, within my tent I was cozy and comfortable and dry.

There was always water in my flasks, which I would fill and carry back with me in the evenings from the dining tent, and light from my lantern by which to read and write and organize my gear for the next day, and bolts and hangers from which to suspend my waders and coats to dry while I slept.

It was a profound place to sleep, and most nights it would rain softly for a few hours, the whispering patter that resonated through the walls as comforting and rejuvenating as the sleep itself. It was vintage sleep, deep and whole and guileless, even after the most trying days casting large flies and heavy sink-tips into the occasional rain squalls that bore upriver off the sea. And then there was the wind.

The Wind. It would begin to build, the mere breath of a breeze, days and even weeks before gaining maturity somewhere out along the steppes of Siberia far to the west. It would then turn and fling itself across the Bering Sea in one great, sweeping gesture of fury and flight, crashing headlong across mountainous waves churned into froth by its own malice, constantly swirling so as to maintain and magnify its effect on the defenseless continent to the east protected only by tundra and grass and threads of a forest dwarfed by the elements, and whose initial mountain defenses lay eighty miles inland.

And then some insidious seam of its wrath would begin probing the coastline, searching for any weakness it could detect. Like biting salt spray in a fresh wound, it would finally discover an opening that fit its purpose and plunge its cold, flaming edge headlong upriver, making its way around and across the sinuous bends of this otherwise peaceful watercourse, where it would then rip the river's surface into a penetrating spray that sought any imperfection it could find in my coat and hood.

It would even work its way behind the polarized glasses that shielded my eyes from its anger and the penetrating glare of the light as I stood facing it, breathing in Siberia in all its bitterness.

Still I persisted, casting into its teeth, my fly line hugging the thin cushion of relatively stable air between the surface of the river and the wind's exposed underbelly. Sometimes my cast flew smoothly out over the surface, its tight, looping thrust remaining intact as it delivered the fly to the exact point I had targeted. But sometimes the wind would discover my treachery and catch my line in mid-course and crash down hard upon it in its resentment, spoiling the precision of the line's tight, surgical arch and forcing me to cast anew.

It was at these moments of perfect imperfection and chaos that I realized the entire universe is still struggling in one great act of giving birth, to what end or beginning I could not fathom. Except to know that, once completed, it would indeed be as the Creator originally intended, unencumbered by the wind and the quaking earth and other such processes of repair under whose influence it presently exists, pristine in every detail and free from the forces that even now interfere with its forming. At such times as these, I longed for the day's end and looked past my obligatory supper to the quiet hour when I could return to my tent and my books and my sleep.

*T**he Sleep*. I prepared carefully for sleep, making certain all my gear and clothing for the next morning were in order and could easily be found when I awoke in the thin light of dawn. I made sure that anything I might need during the night was at hand on the small table just outside the mosquito netting above my head.

There was really very little I might require were I to temporarily awaken – just my glasses and flashlight, and my little notebook and pen and one of my water flasks and watch, for I did like to know how close dawn had crept if I awoke during the night, and more importantly, how much sleep remained.

I would place the spare coat that had become Leota's bed on the floor beside me and then lift down the mosquito netting that Shasta had draped over itself as she made my bed during the day, making certain it was securely tucked in around the foot and back of the mattress where it butted up against the wall. Then I would crawl into bed and pull the netting down around the outside and over my feet and head. My old stocking cap and open-finger gloves were tucked beneath the pillow, and I would slip them on and pull the covers up around my shoulders and would most likely be asleep before Leota had stopped circling and settled into her own bed.

I slept long and I slept deep, sometimes catching and recatching the same trout and grayling and innocent salmon I had caught during the day, there alone with Leota and the soft rain just outside my dreams. I was always aware of Leota's gentle breathing as she slept, and sometimes my hand would find its way outside the mosquito netting and she would awaken and nuzzle it and I would scratch her head or cup my fingertips into the hollow at the base of her ears that all good dogs have, and it would remind me of Betsy, my little Brittany.

Betsy and Carly had overlapped by a year and a half, and I still have films of them playing together when Betsy was old and grey-muzzled and Carly's hair was just beginning to curl. I had named Betsy after a dog for whom I had great respect, and Carly, of course, after my father.

Mary Jane and I had brought Betsy home as a puppy on the first Friday evening we had lived in our very first house. That night she'd slept alone in her new kennel, and the next morning she had been extremely happy to see me. Later that day I had taken a picture of her in the front yard, such as it was, sitting in the straw beside a small, freshly planted oak tree.

Thirteen years later, on the *last* weekend we'd lived in that house, the grass was rich and thick where once there had been only straw, and the pin oak was now twenty-five or thirty feet tall. And on that last Saturday morning, I had carried my little friend a mile across the south face of Bluff Mountain and buried her high near the summit overlooking the valley where our footsteps cannot be numbered.

I buried her above a stream surrounded by laurel and rhododendron in full bloom, in a place she and I had discovered years earlier when we were both still nearly pups. We had hunted through that swale countless times over the intervening years, sometimes pausing there to eat our lunch and have a short nap, and often we had shared a deep drink together shoulder to shoulder at the same pool where now I knelt alone and washed my arms and hands after I had pulled the rich, moist soil over her and firmly pressed it down.

She had died with her dignity. She had died in my hands, *my* head against *her* head as I whispered *"it's okay ..."* over and over in her ear and grimaced in a useless attempt to hold back tears as Dr. Williams loosened the tourniquet and emptied the quieting drug into the vein in her foreleg, and for one long lingering moment her life had passed through mine to mingle with the lives of those who together we had hunted and together we had loved. And then I was alone.

Now as I lay here in the darkness scratching Leota behind the ear, I realized that midnight had come and gone, and once again it was the fourteenth day of July. I smiled as I noted that life does indeed have its symmetry, and I quietly whispered *". . . happy birthday Be'sy Dog."*

Sometimes an idea or a fragment of a poem would nudge me far enough into consciousness to compel me to reach outside the mosquito netting for my pen and the little lined pocket journal I carried nearly everywhere, and in the morning when I would try to decipher what I had written, it was often difficult to read.

I would awaken gradually in the gathering light seeping through the warm inner walls and reach up and out through the netting at my head and feel for my watch, and it seemed always to read 4:53 or 4:54.

For a while I would drift aimlessly between sleep and the waiting river until a question or thought would begin to gather itself in earnest.

Then I would realize where I was and why I was here, and eventually the insistent river would begin to call, or I would hear Leota shuffling her feet impatiently at the door.

I would sit up and carefully begin to disentangle myself from the warm covers and the mosquito netting and my dreams, and eventually my stocking feet would find the wooden floor and I would stand and stretch and ease outside into the chilled Alaska dawn, where the mosquitoes were always happy to see me.

Stepping back inside the warm tent, I would then get dressed and gather my meager gear for the day ahead, slip into waders and make my way with Leota down the trail through the willows and cottonwoods to breakfast and the boat. We would spend the day on the river with the salmon and the trout and the eagles and the great Alaskan bears.

In the evening I would return to my tent.

CHAPTER 25

MADONNA AND CHILD

"I laid a cast across the current to the far bank,
well above the sunken snag, and quickly threw an upstream mend
into the line so as to give the fly plenty of time to sink . . ."

We were less than fifty yards down Schnittle's when we spotted them, two sets of tracks, big bear, little bear, Madonna and Child. But we were already too far along the winding S-shaped entrance of the narrow channel to turn back against the deep, winding current.

Schnittle's Channel is fifteen miles upriver from where the Kanektok empties into the Bering Sea in southwestern Alaska. I do not know who Schnittle is or was or what it might mean. At the time I didn't even know it was the name of this sinuous side stream in which we now found ourselves.

You see, it wasn't just the presence of the tracks that alerted us; it was the fact that there were actually *two* sets of the same twin tracks. One set was at least a day old and already well-weathered and water-pocked by the morning drizzle. But the other was fresh –*very* fresh – with every grain of gravel and every clot of sand crisp and in its place and we knew the grizzlies must be close, for the rain had stopped less than an hour earlier.

It was obvious the pair was using this run on a daily basis and were not merely occasional visitors like ourselves. The short, thick brush that lined the channel came right to the water's edge and even overhung it in places, with the gravel bars on the inside bends the only relief in the tight, twisting flow. It was here beside the bear tracks that we stepped out of the boat and I began making my first exploratory casts into a deep pocket along the far bank as Matt held the boat in place twenty yards upstream. We should be all right, so long as we communicated clearly to Mama that we were here and weren't trying to sneak up on them and that we meant her and the love of her life no harm.

We spoke loudly, repeatedly calling *"Hey bear!"* as we rounded each narrow bend in the channel, and Matt rattled the steel anchor chain against the bottom of the boat every minute or so. As the channel began to straighten and widen slightly, we could see farther downstream with each cast, and somewhere our concentration on the trout overcame our concern with the proximity of the mother and her cub as we continued to cast and call. And then she was there.

And we *knew* she was there; we could smell her, the wind swirling through the low willows and cottonwoods carrying her scent to us. It was a strong, close smell, a combination of musk and feces and rotting salmon flesh that was overpowering in its thickness and intensity . . . and then it was gone. And Matt and I just looked at each other as we continued speaking to her, our overriding focus still on the trout.

I had yet to coax a strike here, so we decided to change flies from a smolt to an egg-and-flesh pattern. The run had straightened out more or less, so we left the boat along a shoal where the water flowed smooth and uninterrupted for a hundred yards or so before it came to a left-hand bend, where the first rainbow of the morning hit.

It struck on the near side of a sunken snag, about three-quarters of the way across the run where the water ran dark and swift beneath the outer bend. I had initially intended to work my way to the far side of this snag and then send the fly deep to search the distant undercut bank beyond. But first I'd drifted it along the *near* side, really more out of obligation than anticipation, where the trout surprised me.

She was about twenty inches, beautifully patterned with the signature soft-edged, ebony dapples that defined her as one of the Kanektok's leopard rainbows, and she took me thirty yards downstream to the head of the next good run before I could bring her to hand and release her.

Already well-positioned for this next hole, I cast across to where an even smaller side channel fed in, and halfway through the second drift another good rainbow tried to take my fly away from me.

This one went airborne immediately, and five minutes later and thirty more yards downstream we finally came to an understanding. Matt eased the net beneath her, then removed the little barbless hook from the corner of her mouth and sent her on her way. I made one more cast into the last bend before Schnittle's fed back out into the main channel two hundred yards below, and again one of the Kanektok's legendary rainbows fell for it, this one well over twenty-two inches.

Now the channel became wider and flatter and much more shallow, and we knew we had passed the truly good trout lies. So as Matt headed back upstream to retrieve the boat, I moved up with him to the snag where the first trout had hit.

As I said, I had initially marked the *far* side of this sunken log as the most likely place for a really big rainbow to be holding. So now I laid a cast across the current to the opposite bank, well above the snag, and quickly threw an upstream mend into the line to give the fly plenty of time to sink deep before it got to the sweet spot directly across from me, fully aware that there was a better-than-even chance it would never make it past the log without getting hung up.

And that's precisely what happened.

Once I realized I couldn't pull the fly free without breaking it off, I made a big, looping false cast well beyond the snag with the upper portion of my line in an effort to put back-pressure on the embedded fly and free it, but to no avail. I really did not want to lose that fly here, for Matt invests a great deal of time and care in tying these beautiful patterns.

And so I tried the last thing I could think of.

With the wind at my back, I moved deeper into the run, as far as I could go, until I was more than three-quarters of the way across the little channel. There, I was finally able to reach across and barely get the end of my fly rod beyond the far side of the old snag. Then just as Matthew arrived with the boat, I gave the rod tip a firm upward flip and the fly flew free, and at that precise moment from less than twenty yards directly in front of me the mother grizzly suddenly spoke, issuing a loud, guttural and very emphatic *"Woof!"*

The translation was instantaneous and oh so easy to understand:

"Okay, I have been listening to you for the past hour and smelling you for even longer, and for the last several minutes I have been watching you and have tried to be as patient and polite as possible . . . but now it seems you are intent on crossing to my *side of the stream and I have this youngster here with me, you see, who is the absolute joy of my life and this is about as far as I am comfortable allowing you to approach us, Southern Boy.*

Your move."

Her communique was very well thought out and succinct and quite professionally presented, and it was suddenly and chillingly clear *exactly* how the board was set: she was lying unseen with her cub less than twenty yards in front of me in a dense and slightly elevated clump of willows. She had obviously been watching us from this position as we fished past her, and so long as we were on *our* side of the stream, she had been content to stay on hers. I'd not been in front of her for very long at all as I had played the first trout earlier, for it had quickly taken me downstream and away from her and hers. It wasn't until I had returned and waded into the stream to retrieve my fly, and then presumed to cross nearly all the way to *her* side, that she'd felt compelled to express herself.

But expressing herself had cost her something – *she* knew it and *I* knew it – for she had now given away her position to me, whom she obviously perceived as a potential threat. I could sense that she was feeling much more vulnerable now than she had before she'd spoken, which by default meant that she had likely just moved to Defcon Three.

I knew if she came, she'd be coming downhill with a full head of steam, and here I was standing less than twenty yards from her in water up to my chest, armed only with my little six-weight, a tiny box of flies and a small wooden landing net. It was clear to all concerned that the next communication, and therefore the whole outcome of this encounter, was now entirely up to me.

urprisingly, I felt no fear and very little immediate threat from her. I was in fact somewhat reassured by her eloquence and courtesy, for had she been so inclined she could already have taken me out without ever bothering to formally introduce herself. She was plainly an exceptionally well-educated and calculating mother bear, and so long as my response to her was correct and clearly communicated, we should all come out of this relatively intact – and perhaps even have some interesting stories to share with our respective friends and families.

So long as I made the correct next move.

And so I slumped. I slumped her as good a slump as I knew how to slump, my arms and shoulders as wide as I could make them and my head and fly rod lowered in respect, and without either looking directly at her or turning my back to her, I moved casually, oh so casually, away from her and out of the water, trying to express neither haste that might incite an instinctive charge response, nor fear and weakness that would in any way dampen or dilute her obvious caution.

Looking behind me, I could see that Matt was doing the same, pepper spray in one hand and the gunnel of the boat in the other as we moved away from her together, slowly and deliberately easing down the shallow edge of the run with the boat in tow.

As we looked around, we could see *our* tracks over *her* tracks and those of her cub. And by the time we swung out of Schnittle's and back into the main channel of the Kanektok, I suspect she was probably explaining to her yearling what had just occurred and how he should behave when next these foul-smelling beasts from downriver arrive.

CHAPTER 26

THE INTENTIONAL GRAYLING

"It was a marvelous morning, one I shall treasure
for as long as I have memory."

W hen last I'd fished the Kanektok, I had caught one of the largest grayling anyone there had ever seen. It was my very first grayling, at least twenty inches long and wearing colors that I knew only from the tropics, and carrying its tall signature dorsal fin like the national flag of the entire Grayling nation.

At the time I had been fishing for rainbows, but it had not hit like a rainbow and it had not fought like a rainbow, and when we'd finally brought it to net, it had taken longer for *me* to recover than it had the fish. For though I had come here to Alaska for Pacific salmon and rainbows, it had been grayling I had secretly longed to catch, and now I had finally fulfilled the dream of childhood to one day fish for these true spirits of the north country.

Or so at first it had seemed.

I tell you this not to boast, but rather to apologize. For as the evening of the catching wore on and my guide Matt kept telling the others in camp about the giant grayling and everyone continued to marvel at the photos and congratulate me on my supposed accomplishment, I grew more and more uncomfortable, both with the accolades and the circumstances in which I had caught the great fish.

For you see, I had not actually been fishing for grayling when he hit.

In my own mind and intention I had been focused on rainbows as I'd drifted the fly across the angular lip of the ledge and into the deep run that fanned out below.

Matt had known there was the occasional grayling to be found in this stretch of the river, but knowing how badly I wanted to catch one, he had not dared mention to me that this might be good grayling water. But even *he* did not expect one so large to be holding in this particular run.

We had been looking for them elsewhere for days, primarily in the side channels and flat water that fringe the broad, braided river, while we'd concentrated on salmon and trout. But we had never expected one to be lying where this one had lain.

And so as the evening wore on and people kept wandering into the community tent and coming over to the camp laptop to view the digital photographs we had taken of the fish before we'd released him, I grew increasingly uncomfortable with my supposed accomplishment, not to mention the congratulations I was now receiving, especially from the other guides, who themselves shook their heads and swore they had never seen such a huge grayling.

Surely they knew, as I knew, it was dumb luck that I had caught such a large and unlikely fish in such a large and unlikely run; this was my very first grayling, and there had been no grayling skill involved on my part, let alone grayling *intention*.

It had been sheer luck; the fish should have been in the small flat water in the side channels and along the edges.

I tried to be magnanimous and not appear unappreciative. But that evening as I made my way up the trail to my tent I felt small and alone, knowing that despite the record-class fish now tallied to my credit, I had still not fished for grayling. Not for real.

Now I was once more back on the Kanektok, this time with my friend Josh Young as guide, filled yet again with the spirit of Alaska, my longing for the mystery fish of the north still there and empty, yet strong and unspoken.

Josh understood. I am certain he did. Josh is not only a world-class guide but a very intuitive friend, and as we motored far upstream he ran barely at half-speed and would slow down even more each time we'd near the mouth of one of the river's side channels, where we would dissect the tailing pools with our eyes searching for any vague evidence of the surface dapples that might betray the presence of grayling.

As I said, Josh understood.

And finally, not far below where the Bat Channel and the Old Main Channel converge, Josh eased the boat onto a gravel bar alongside a broad expanse of bear grass that lined a small side lead winding out of the willows. Leaving the boat anchored in the gravel, we crossed the mouth of the lead where it fed into the main river.

I followed Josh upstream with my little three-weight along a very well-used bear trail, reaching out and letting the dew-laden tips of the tall grass brush against my down-turned palms.

And when we rounded the concealing right-hand bend, there lay before us a broad, flat pool whose coy face was dotted with the tell-tale markings of rising grayling.

Josh turned and smiled, and it was a knowing smile, as though he'd had this place in mind all along. Grayling are still comparatively scarce here on the Kanektok, having been heavily impacted a few years earlier by some sort of virus that swept their numbers. But here they were before us, calmly cruising up and down and across the pool, delicately sipping something unseen from the still surface that reflected the blue Alaska sky in all its morning splendor.

Quietly and discreetly we crossed the bar that held back the channel and formed the pool above us. Now we could see them clearly – little grayling, dainty and demure and very private. I knelt low in the water with Josh behind me, and my fly line rolled smoothly through the cool morning air, discreetly depositing a tiny #22 Griffith's Gnat lightly onto the dark mirror surface eight feet above where a ringlet had appeared seconds earlier.

Another ring suddenly surrounded my fly, and I struck lightly but firmly, the little three-weight perfectly protecting the delicate 7X tippet, and I felt the pressure of my first intentional grayling.

He swirled downstream, then turned on the line and bolted back up into the head of the pool, and for a moment I nearly lost the direct tension to the little barbless fly sitting lightly in the edge of his lip.

But finally he turned back toward me and I worked him close and then slipped my hand into the water and beneath his side, lifting him only as far as the surface as I eased the tiny hook from his lip. Once free, he bolted back into the deep water along the outside of the bend without needing to be revived.

He was barely nine inches long according to my hand-span, but he was a sure-enough grayling, intentionally sought and intentionally caught, and now at last I was able to consider myself a true grayling fisherman. It was a grand feeling and a grand morning. And so, with a legendary Alaska river filled with legendary Alaska salmon just downstream, we spent . . . excuse me, we *invested* . . . the entire morning here in this diminutive side channel with these diminutive fish.

It was a marvelous morning, one I shall treasure for as long as I have memory. I finally offered the fly rod to Josh and took the camera he'd been carrying for me, and I began working my way up and down the side channel, watching for bears and eagles and photographing Josh as he fished.

In the end we caught grayling so small as to barely fill the palms of our hands, and we caught grayling as large as twelve or thirteen inches. But it wasn't the size that mattered; it was the simple fact that they were *grayling* and that we were here of our own intention surrounded by giant salmon and great bears and overwhelming country, catching these little elven fish on their own terms.

And when the morning was done and our souls were filled to overflowing, there was no longer the emptiness in my spirit made emptier by the big accidental grayling. I was fine, just as I have been ever since we left that little side lead through the tall grass, not far downstream from where the Bat Channel and the Old Main Channel converge.

And where a small part of my soul still haunts the bear trails of the upper Kanektok.

CHAPTER 27

THE DAY WE
BLEW UP VIEW HILL

---

*"Trout always have a way
of elevating the spirits of those they touch,
especially fine young researchers like David and me . . . "*

O kay, let me be perfectly clear and state right up front: We never, *ever* intended to do any harm to anything or anyone; all we wanted was simply to catch a few trout and build a small, innocuous bomb.

I can assure you, it was all very innocent, more a *"research"* project, if you will. You see, we did a lot of research back when we were in our late single digits, my cousin David and I. Like how far down the hill from Flat Rock each of us could sail one of its signature flat rocks (remind me sometime to tell you how the place got its name).

Besides, how could we possibly have known that some little kid would have been so irresponsible as to be playing alone in his back yard directly below us on such a beautiful and inviting springtime Saturday morning when there were all those perfectly good rocks to be flown from above?

We did, in fact, add quite a bit to our respective bodies of knowledge from that single experiment, and not just about the relative aerodynamic characteristics of flat planes of sedimentary stone moving at varying angles and velocities against the resistance of the lower atmosphere; we actually once and for all settled the often-debated issue of which of us could run faster, as well as adding to our ever-expanding vocabularies with some quite interesting and heretofore unknown words and phrases from the aforementioned irresponsible little kid's father, who to his credit exhibited commendable speed and nimbleness for such a large man in street shoes. Still, we were a good deal quicker going down the *far* side than he was coming up the *near* side, and all things considered we thought it all turned out pretty well in the end, though we did come to miss our regular visits over to Flat Rock.

Then there was the summer afternoon when in one of our good-deed-doing modes we decided to test the relative merits of our very own designs for wooden swords. David's had a thick, rounded blade and mine a flatter, slightly curved and much more elegant profile. There was this patch of tall, thick-stemmed, broadleaf weeds growing beside our next-door-neighbor Mr. Atwood's garage, which was a perfect, not to mention convenient, subject for our experiment, giving us the opportunity to carry out extensive research with our individual self-made weapons, as well as the chance to perform yet another in our legendary line of good deeds by clearing out that patch of whatever it was that kept growing larger as summer wore on.

I distinctly recall David and I discussing the fact that it was very odd of Mr. Atwood not to have taken care of the problem himself, since he was otherwise known for being such a meticulous man with his yard and garden. Anyhow, we figured he just hadn't gotten around to it yet and so, it being late in the summer, we decided to do the job for him.

The brutality of our coordinated attack was complete and merciless, punctuated with some of the more colorful expressions we had learned from our Saturday afternoon matinee trips uptown to the Clinch Valley Theater and even a couple of the words and phrases we had picked up from that little kid's father over at Flat Rock. We left not the smallest stem standing, with green shredded leaves and red bleeding stalks strewn hither and yon across the face of the garage wall and well out into the yard. Our blood ran high from the adrenaline that was always certain to accompany such successful research, and we would have, should have, cleaned it all up right then and there. But we figured that if we were to leave the evidence lying about for a while and mosey on into the house for a good belt of Kool-Aid, someone important just might notice our well-intended efforts and perhaps say something like, "Hey, who are the good-deed-doers who did away with that old patch of weeds?"

At the time, Dad and Verlin were out in the den lambasting one another with stories of catching trout and hunting deer and shooting squirrels and rabbits and grouse, with Mom and Ann sternly admonishing them that anything they killed in that den had better be taken outside to clean.

We had heard it all many times before and really weren't paying that much attention until we noticed the heavy knock on the door and heard Mr. Atwood's voice, rather animated it seemed for such an otherwise calm and orderly man. David and I were looking straight at each other with sickeningly self-congratulatory grins on our little freckled faces, patiently and self-righteously awaiting the praise we were certain was forthcoming, when we heard him utter the word "*Rhubarb*."

I can still remember how cramped it was down there underneath that little wooden platform out by the crest of the hill with the spiders and slugs and snakes and protruding nails. It wasn't nearly large enough for *one* culprit to hide beneath, much less both of us, especially with Dad's booming voice calling my humble and growing humbler name in a way I had not previously heard it called and in a manner that would surely have dislodged the most well-concealed Knight Errant in Tazewell County.

David and I were soon facing the Inquisitors, trying to explain how otherwise responsible adults such as those before whom we now stood really ought to exercise better judgement than to leave innocent plants growing unattended, not to mention unlabeled, in an environment where blessed little cherubs such as ourselves might conceivably make such purely unintended errors in botanical identification during one of our otherwise noble endeavors. I think I may even recall violins playing plaintively somewhere behind us as we made our presentation.

At any rate, to this day I still have an aversion to the word "rhubarb," and of all the confections that have been prepared over the years by the more culinarily inclined members of our family, I still don't think that either David or I have ever developed much of a taste for rhubarb pie.

I would prefer to not even discuss the time we broke into David's neighbors' house while they were away on vacation (just to make sure no one had broken into David's neighbors' house while they were away on vacation), or how once in the heat of debate we made an impromptu test of the physical effects of a conveniently placed garden stake on each others' upper skeletal structure. But back to our research.

We figured that since we had now outgrown such basic and childish pursuits as rock-sailing and wooden weapons and introductory espionage and the applied dynamics of pine lumber on flesh and bone, it was time to focus our ever-expanding repertoire of intentions upon something more substantive.

I'm not quite certain which of us first had the idea that the science of Pyrotechnics could be an interesting field of study, but I'm relatively certain it must have been David. It was getting close to Christmas, so late one snowy Friday evening down in the basement we took a few of the firecrackers we'd been hoarding and carefully disassembled them, meticulously flattening out the gray-powdered layers of paper and then stuffing them into a small thread box we had clandestinely appropriated from Mom and Ann's sewing shop. Then we wove the fuses together as best we could until finally we had the makings of something we thought might actually produce both sound *and* fury.

By then it was dark, and so we decided to postpone the final phase of our experiment until morning, since we did not want the blinding flash and explosion that we were certain we'd produce to attract the wrong sort of attention. In our line of work, discretion was a very important component of effective research.

The next morning we sneaked . . . excuse me, *took* . . . the device out from behind David's dad's tool box where we had stashed it the night before so that no irresponsible little kids might find it, and we headed out the basement door and up around Mrs. Leslie's house to the steep back side of View Hill where we felt no residences or civilians would be in undue peril. Obviously being the more responsible of the two, I carried the matches myself, and we did a couple of practice runs as to how to light the long, knotted fuse and get the various parts of our respective anatomies the heck as far across the steep wooded slope as possible, away from the impending conflagration.

Finally, the moment came to do the deed for real, and as soon as I lit the end of the fuse, I swung up and around and away from the device and straight into David, who had quietly come up from behind to make a few impromptu observations of his own. Immediately we both went down in a heap, and I found it increasingly difficult to get back on my feet as we slipped farther and farther down the steep, wooded hillside with David clawing at my coat in an equally desperate attempt to get back up himself.

I think I even remember one or more of us blowing furiously in the general direction of the fuse in a futile attempt to extinguish it. But by then there were so many other things flashing through my mind, most of them autobiographical, that I'm not entirely certain that the huffing and puffing had any effect at all except to better oxygenate and thus speed up the creeping flame, which proceeded to burn right up to the edge of the box where there was a sudden small and anemic *puff*.

I think a couple of birds may have stopped chirping for a few seconds as they casually glanced in our direction, but that was about the extent of it, and as we untangled ourselves from the ground and the vines and each other, we commented on the fact that perhaps we needed to expand our thinking as well as our process. But never in our wildest imagination did we ever intend to produce such a *LARGE* explosion, and certainly not one that would eventually be seen by so much of the county . . . but I'm getting ahead of myself.

You see, View Hill did not get its name by accident. It was named "View Hill" because from it you could see all the way down to Riverjack, out toward Four Way, then over the top of the schoolyard and downtown Tazewell, clear around the Peak and nearly across into Thompson Valley. It really *was* some view; that's one reason Verlin had moved his family up there in the first place.

But the same geology that gave View Hill its magnificent panorama had also placed one very steep slope smack on the back side of David's house. *(Note to self: consider rewording that phrase " . . . smack on the back side.")* This precipitous slope grew mainly scrub cedar and oak and tangled vines atop steeply angled shale and was of absolutely no logical use at all to anyone with innocuous intentions . . . which made it a perfect place for a hideout or escape route or, as was now the case, an ideal explosives research area, perilously steep though it was.

So one lovely and fateful Saturday afternoon in early autumn following an especially fine morning's trout fishing with Dad and Verlin, David and I slinked out the basement door and oozed over the edge of the precipice with matches and rope and gasoline bucket and other assorted implements of research in hand and cautiously worked our way down the tricky slope in our relentless quest for knowledge and understanding.

You see, we had done particularly well trout-fishing that morning. Trout always have a way of elevating the spirits of fine young researchers like David and me, who had been promised it would be the very trout that he and I had caught that morning that Mom and Ann would fry up fresh for everyone's supper that night. We now considered ourselves to be among the nobility, providers-of-meals for our families, standers-in-the-way-of-starvation-and-annihilation. We were the slayers of dragons, friends of dogs and stray ponies, and rescuers of damsels . . . well, maybe forget the damsels, for at that stage of our lives, damsels were still the enemy, Cousin Debbie excepted.

But we were still quite confident that we could handle any ol' dragon who might exercise the poor judgement to rear his oversized sulfuric head anywhere in our immediate vicinity. Especially once we had a firmer grasp on the science of Pyrotechnics.

You have to understand, the back side of View Hill was so steep and thick and tangled that during spring and summer and well into fall, there were places where no light could penetrate the leafy canopy and reach the ground. And therefore, where neither smoke nor flame could escape directly to be seen by unreasonably paranoid and suspicious neighbors or teachers or parents. They all thought we were down there playing mountaineers or cowboys or chess.

We would always build ourselves a little campfire in a small pit we had long ago excavated below an extremely narrow, semi-level ledge, even on such a nice afternoon as this. It had little to do with keeping warm – it's just that deeper and more industrious thoughts, be they scientific, philosophic, artistic or religious, simply couldn't be effectively considered without the aid of a well-endowed campfire. And this afternoon, we clearly had some intense thinking to do.

We meant to start out small and work our way up as we progressed, with at first no more than a gallon or so of gasoline in our open bucket. In addition to the gasoline, we had wooden matches and glass jars of varying sizes and a plastic canister we had borrowed from the garage we were still in the process of cleaning out for Mrs. Leslie. We had even broken apart what was left of our now-dwindling supply of firecrackers and smeared the powdery contents onto a two-foot section of waxed and interwoven kite string that we fondly referred to as our *fuse*.

So with both conspirators present, we precariously laid out all our materials up on that narrow ledge above the campfire, wedging them and the gasoline bucket into position with rocks and sticks and vines and whatever else we could find, and each of us sat down on opposite ends of the ledge and began our final conference.

And I thought everything was coming together quite nicely until David – *I swear it was him* – began casually tugging at one of the small vines that snaked down from the tree he was wedged against, across the slope toward the fire, then uphill, worming its way along that same narrow ledge whereupon rested our matches, our jars, our fuse and our open bucket of gasoline.

The first indication I had that all was not as it should be in the Universe was the clanging of the gasoline bucket as it tipped over toward the fire, followed closely by an amplified *whooosh* and what can only be described as an intense concussion, with leaves and branches and other assorted bits flying in all directions around us and swirling skyward, and that lovely leafy canopy that had so effectively provided us shelter for so long now disappearing into a dark roaring mushroom of blackened flame rolling heavenward in the general direction of the Gates of Pearl.

And David and I just stared at each other with our mouths agape and then looked up through the swirling debris with expressions of terror and amazement and accomplishment as we each clawed at the charred hillside in a desperate, and might I say eventually successful, attempt to halt our downslope momentum. I particularly remember the *terror* part, and how large and artificially white David's eyes seemed to be at the time, though now on further reflection I am sure it was simply their accentuated contrast against his sooty little face.

We could still hear the fireball somewhere above us, continually climbing, and for the briefest moment I thought I heard the sweet sound of angels singing, intermingled with the many exclamations of wonder and bewilderment now beginning to filter in to us though the din from neighbors and family and friends both above and below.

And when we finally came wandering home an hour or so later from the *opposite* side of View Hill, everyone came running up to us asking if we had seen the inferno, and we assured them we had, but we'd been much too busy working on Mrs. Leslie's garage to really pay all that much attention to it, and by the way, when would supper be ready?

The trout Mom and Ann fried up that night were particularly tasty, and David's extended blessing before the meal seemed especially fervent. Our families appeared to be thrilled and relieved to know their precious little ones were safe, though later that evening it occurred to me that Dad and Verlin really hadn't had all that much to say during supper.

But they sure had been looking at us funny.

CHAPTER 28

VERLIN

"I gave him Dad's steelhead rod
after Dad died, and Verlin told me about the last steelhead
my father ever caught with it up on the Betsie . . ."

Maybe it's because we were born in West Virginia. Except for a few misapplied years in my sometimes misspent youth, I have lived in the South ever since I was an eleven-year-old transplant from the coal fields. But if the history and heritage of the South is the Confederacy, then surely my *own* heritage is West Virginia.

I was a misplaced Yankee when we moved to Tennessee and a misplaced Rebel whenever I journeyed back north. Today, I have friends across the planet, including some particularly close friends in the classic quail country of southwest Georgia, who still refer to the War Between the States simply as *"The Northern Aggression."* We have discussed the matter often. But frankly, I have always maintained that West Virginia is the quintessential rebel state, for not only did it secede from the Union, it then managed to secede from the Confederacy as well.

If you are fortunate enough to have been born in West Virginia, you have a mind of your own, and there's not all that much you can do about it. You don't particularly care for crowds; you don't automatically accept another person's opinion as your own; and if you are going to spend any time at all trout fishing with someone, they'd better be pretty upstanding people *and* outdoorsmen, or they're going to get left behind somewhere along the trail and not be asked to come again.

But if by chance you find someone who works for you, and you work for them, you can never again go fishing alone, for they are always a part of the experience, whether they are actually there with you or not.

You sometimes find this sort of relationship among brothers, so long as their understanding of one another resides in the deeper, more sublime recesses of brotherhood. In late autumn after Dad died, my own brother Alan and I spent a cold November night watching the Northern Lights together, and when we tried talking about it a week later as we sat on Debbie's floor back down in southern Michigan, she sat between us, cross-legged and confused, listening as my brother and I spoke in turn about what we had seen and how it had been and how we had each danced alone with our father beneath the stars as Borealis had danced among them. She simply couldn't fathom how we had managed to share the experience, Alan camped alone on a ridge in western Montana, and I by a moonless lake in northern Ontario.

That's simply the way it is when brothers are truly brothers.

But what if there *isn't* a brother with whom to share such a thing? Could you find another person elsewhere? Might you by mere chance come across someone who would knowingly and without hesitation or question take you at face value and leave you gasping for air with stupid jokes that only you and he could possibly understand? Could you ever find someone with whom to share a cup or a poem or a prayer?

Perhaps. If you are either very lucky or very blessed.

Or both.

And so here, I suppose, is finally the place to write about Verlin.

They were actually first cousins, Dad and Verlin. But that's about as far as it went, at least so far as previous relations and social ties were concerned. I'm not entirely sure how close they were as children, though I do know they went to grade school together in Bishop. Verlin later commented to Alan and me about how impressed he had been with Dad even back then, Dad getting B's and C's while Verlin got A's and B's, because, as he said, " . . . *your Dad didn't have any textbooks.*"

Life was hard when they were young. Excuse me, did I say *young*? I'm sorry, for I don't think that either of them ever had much of an opportunity to actually be young. I mean, really *young*. Not having to worry about what was for supper, or even if there would *be* a supper. To giggle wildly and play recklessly and simply be childish. Well at least not until they started trout fishing together after Dad came home from Pearl Harbor and Verlin from Normandy.

I never thought to get the whole story of how they reconnected after the war, but they did, and we are all the better for it. What I do know is that they each came back home to Bishop and went to work at the mine, with Dad dumping coal cars at the tipple and Verlin eventually making his way into the front office. Somewhere along the way they discovered their kindred interests and began trout fishing together. Eventually, Dad became a glass-maker in Tennessee, while Verlin rose to upper management with the coal company in West Virginia. And though they were now separated by more miles than they had been since the war, they were still one another's *true north* and a perfect reflection of each other's soul.

How do you explain to your wife – for that matter, how do you convince *yourself* – that you have found someone who already knows what *you* know and feels what *you* feel? Someone who can share your spectacles and eat your food and who will in turn feed *you* anytime you might be hungry.

From the time David and I were barely old enough to tag along with our fathers, we knew they were pretty much interchangeable. At least they were for us. Verlin would just as readily help me with a tangle or a knot as he would his own son, and so too Dad with David. It is something we reflect on to this day, my cousin and I.

They were *Giants*, our fathers, both in physical stature and in personal character and integrity, as available to each of us as another boy's dad could possibly be. Mind you, I would never have traded fathers with David, though I knew that if the time ever came, as eventually it did, Verlin would be the closest thing to Dad I could hope for.

They were truly *brothers*, if not of the same parentage, then at least of the same spirit, as complementary to one another as two hands clasped in prayer. Theirs was a spirit of mutual admiration and mutual respect and a deep and kindred love for the outdoors. And especially for the trout.

Verlin often didn't much care whether or not he caught a trout for himself, and the older he got the stronger these inclinations grew; he simply loved the fishing. His ultimate fulfillment came in watching one of his kids, or better still one of his grandkids, catch a trout for themselves. He always said that he could tell the true heart and soul of a man simply by spending a day with him on the creek, and more than one meeting or interview has been held on the trout streams he knew so well.

I was nearly ten years old before I realized Verlin wasn't actually my blood uncle. Not that it mattered, for I knew then and I know now that he was as close to Dad as anyone could ever be. When I talked with him, it was as though I were talking with Dad. He was the only one left, you see, who still knew the stories and could tell me what Dad was thinking and just how good a trout fisherman he was.

Verlin knew the places and he knew the songs and could still tell me what I already knew for myself if only I could remember.

I have tried not to write about Verlin's passing, for death is a private matter to men such as he and Dad. So I will say no more than that Verlin died late and he died well.

The evening before he left us, I came straight from the stream to his bedside and we talked trout fishing long into the night. He showed me how to work a deep streamer, sitting up in his hospital bed in his hospital shirt with the plastic tube draining his stricken lung, me sitting before him, the perpetual student, he scribing the air with his silent cast, then rolling the invisible fly rod to his right and deftly dipping the tip, the absent line in his off-hand held in perfect geometry with the imaginary rod, working the fly, mending the line, then swinging it across the current and down, waiting to breathe, waiting for the take, waiting for the strike that never came, calling me now what Dad had called me and telling me the final things he would have me know, sharing the story of he and Dad and their last trip to Michigan.

You see, I had given him Dad's steelhead rod after Dad died, and lately he had given it back to me. And now he told me about the last steelhead my father ever caught with it up on the Betsie. Dad had hooked the great fish in the edge of a long, tailing current below a deeply submerged windfall and had struggled mightily to keep it out of the thick sub-surface tangle of limbs. Verlin had worked his way into the crease below Dad, and together they had been able to coax the fish to the net and had kept it in the water as they removed the tiny hook from its jaw, then revived it and sent it on its way.

I'm glad I wasn't there with them to see it for myself, because the image Verlin portrayed was much more vivid than anything I could ever have hoped to remember on my own. The fact that I don't know all the details of how he and Dad caught that steelhead really isn't much of a loss, for what is important is that they caught it.

Together.

That it was Dad who held the rod didn't make the fish any more *his* than Verlin's. For I am certain that the most important part of the whole thing for him was not the *fish* but the other *fisherman* who was there to share the experience.

And now I simply cannot help but wonder if the Northern Lights danced for them that night.

– CHAPTER 29 –

FISHING IN THE BLOOD OF CHRIST

"He knew that if he
were ever to fish again he must fish now,
even though he was not here to fish."

By the time he found his voice as a painter, he knew it was probably too late to do all that much with it. When it came, it was Sargent – *John Singer Sargent* – along with Winslow Homer and Bob Kuhn and Vincent Van Gogh who best typified how he would like to have painted, had he lived his life to paint and therefore painted the life he wished he had lived.

He loved painting. And drawing. And reading. More than reading, he loved reading good writing – real, honest *"reach down your throat and grab you by your good parts and turn you inside-out"* writing.

Still more, he loved *writing*.

But now it was too late to be a painter, a real painter, and he knew it. In fact, he had already done just about all he would ever do, and whatever he might someday leave behind as evidence of his living was for the most part already painted, already drawn, already written, and he was mostly all the artist he would ever be. But not nearly the artist he might have been, and he knew *that* too.

It was a crime to have spent so much of his life merely on the living. And now there was really nothing he could do, nothing he could say, nothing he could think, to change it. At most, there was enough time left to do the best he still could do, he thought, as he sat there waiting for daylight in the little cabin on the upper edge of the valley, high in the Sangre de Cristo mountains.

It had all seemed more or less worthwhile to him at the time – even responsible. Only now was he beginning to realize what it had cost him, what he had spent instead of investing, what he had wasted in the living and the dreaming and the good intentions of what he'd meant to do and meant to be someday.

Someday. *Someday*.

When would it come? Someday.

Would it come . . . *Someday?* What he had actually been, what he had actually done, paled in comparison to what he *might* have been, what he might have done, what he might still have left to do to mark the way for those who may eventually find his trail.

But for now it was still dark outside, and as he sat alone waiting for daybreak next to the small lamp whose dim yellow light barely covered his little pocket journal, he glanced up toward the door and caught his own reflection in the glass, and for a moment he didn't recognize the pale image reflected back to him from the high New Mexico night.

But indeed it was himself he saw, and it really wasn't all that bad, so long as he didn't look too closely. His brother was still asleep in the bunk in the back room, and soon first light would begin feathering the eastern rim, and there would be yet another day to do what had not yet been done. He capped his pen and tucked it into his shirt pocket, then closed the little green journal and slipped it into his coat.

His fly rod was ready. And so too, he hoped, was he.

When you know that the best thing you can do in life is to take the thing you love most and make it possible for her to leave and live without you, and you know that the only thing that could possibly hurt more than freeing her would be keeping her and binding her to yourself, it is like having to take a dull knife and cut out your own heart. Yet this is what he'd had to do. And now she was gone, the little curly haired girl who had always been and always would be his reason for being.

The last trout he'd caught, he had caught here with her a year earlier, just a few days before he'd taken her away to college. She had been so excited that morning as they left together, her little butterfly wings now full and mature and eager to fly. And now he knew that if he were ever to fish again he must fish today, even though he was not here to fish.

H e was here hunting elk with his brother. His bow and leather quiver of arrows stood waiting for him in the corner where he'd set them last night when they'd come off the mountain. But for now the mountain, the bow, even his brother would have to wait, for he had claimed this one morning as his own to fish.

As he stepped out of the cabin and into the crisp still air of the starlit night, he could hear the gurgling murmur of the creek far down the valley. The moon hovered just above the horizon, the muted trunks of the aspens that edged the high meadows stood like empty shadows on the edge of darkness, and he could sense the stream long before he saw its first pale reflection. An elk bugled from two ridges north.

This morning he wanted to fish for trout more than he wanted to catch a trout, and the muscle memory that defines a proper cast slowly awoke from its long dormancy as he gradually recalled what it felt like for a fine fly rod to load.

It was good to remember – to know he still possessed what his father had given him as a boy and which he in turn had passed along to his daughter, and for the briefest moment he didn't feel quite so old. His father hadn't seemed old either, but looking back, he realized he *had* been old. Still, old was a good thing to be, so long as you didn't look too closely at what it meant to *be* old.

Or better still, if you did.

H e'd once looked forward to this time of life as an opportunity to do more of the things he had always wanted to do. But now that he was actually here, he saw it for what it really was, the definitive entry into the final phase of his physical self.

Beyond that, he could not see.

He sometimes felt that perhaps the real living had already been done, in the preparation of youth and the building of a career and through the rich and enervating experiences of fatherhood. And now he would much rather go back and live it all again than move forward into the time at hand. *If only I had understood,* he thought.

But what, if anything, could he do now to *begin* to understand, to prepare for what his father had once called "the last great adventure?"

For most of his life he had tried to anticipate what lay ahead. *So why not now?* And suddenly he realized what was going to happen:

He was going to die.

Just as his father had died before him, he was actually going to *die.*

Oddly enough, once realized and accepted, it was all right; it's okay to die, so long as you know what it means and you are as ready as you can be for what comes next. It's simply the progression of being.

What an interesting prospect, he thought.

Once considered, it was almost ironic, as though a great burden had been lifted, and he instinctively understood that since there was nothing he could do to change the dying, he might as well experience it to the fullest. After all, he knew that barring accident or sudden illness, his dying was not immediately imminent, though its absolute certainty, now realized, would be his constant companion for as long as he lived.

The first trout of the rest of his life hit beneath a low, grassy overhang, deep along the tail end of an outside run just as daylight was beginning to feather the valley. It hit a #18 Royal Wulff and ran upstream into the head of the pool and deep beneath the grass along the far bank.

It tried to stay there, gave it all it had, but the pressure of the rod was simply too much and the little brookie was soon brought to hand and released. And now here at 9000 feet, high in the Sangre de Cristo, the *Blood of Christ* mountains, he felt that the first part of a long journey had finally come to an end.

It was a beginning. Or perhaps more importantly, a *continuation*.

Whatever it was, it had all played out in less than four minutes in the low morning light that was now bringing the world around him to life.

He had expected this to be an event of proportion and gravitas, and for now he felt that this one trout was perhaps enough. Still, he wasn't entirely sure whether he wanted to continue fishing or head back to the cabin, where he knew his brother and his bow would be waiting for him.

He made one more cast. Perhaps he made two. But he knew he had already done what he'd come here to do, and if he were looking for more he would have to find it somewhere deeper than this little stream, somewhere higher than this high valley floor. He slipped the point of the hook into the cork handle of his fly rod, and as he turned to go he could see the rim of the ridge above him beginning to glow as the sunrise on its far side continued to build.

The cabin itself was less than a mile up the valley, but he had a sudden, compelling urge to go and meet the sun face to face. And so he bore east, across the broad, frosty meadow and into the black timber at the base of the ridge. Darkness again enveloped him as he worked his way up the steep slope, moving by the feel of the fallen leaves beneath his feet and the fleeing night breezes on the side of his face.

And then he saw it, a bright, burning light not so far above, and he laid his fly rod down in the leaves and began to quicken his pace, his breath coming labored in the rarified air.

He sensed a sudden and nearly overwhelming compulsion to pray, to communicate with the Infinite in a way they could both understand, and when he tried, the prayer seemed to return to him with a clarity and presence beyond anything he'd ever known, and he found himself doing more listening than telling.

216

Colors and patterns became increasingly pure and dynamic, and for the first time he found he could see the individual mauves and corals and teals in the morning sky around him. Even the warm blood that coursed his veins felt vital and alive as he finally reached the ridgetop overlooking the next valley to the east.

He knew this was a place both in space and time that he would always remember, to what end he could not tell. Yet telling, for the moment, was not important. After all, he thought, we are even now creatures of the Infinite, surely having existed in God's intention long before He chose to express us in any physical form.

We tarry here but for a few million breaths, our dying the last reality of consciousness and the first fact of the Eternal, leaving us to wonder about the true nature of this relatively brief physical interlude that we vaguely perceive as *life*.

Is it a grand reward for something well done or well intended in some other realm? Or is it instead a harsh and stunning consequence of something gone terribly wrong? Or is it simply a necessary transition from one side of Eternity to the other, a spiritual womb of sorts in which our true essence is formed and refined in preparation for a greater purpose which we are, for the time being, able to perceive only through the tantalizing hints that God has written for us in the timeless languages of science and scripture and mathematics?

But he had no answers . . . nor were answers required. The questions themselves would have to suffice. For now he was still a part of the *physical* world. And as he looked around he knew he was in a lovely place, a place of timeless perfection, if only for this one brief moment.

He also knew that the perceived perfection of where he now stood paled in comparison to where he might someday stand, just as surely as he knew that the single trout he had caught minutes earlier still swam in the little stream far below. He closed his eyes and could feel its body undulating in his hands as it had awaited its freedom from a brief captivity, just as he could sense his own spiritual undulations and his own pending release into the reality he had just discovered.

It was no longer important how many days or years he might be able to tag onto his physical existence, for he now saw life as a temporary state, pre-natal to the Greater Reality that inevitably awaits us all.

The night had become light around him, the darkness dissolving into the past where it rightly belonged and where it would forever remain, so long as he did not call it forward. Death was no longer to be feared, nor was it to be embraced; it was simply an inevitable passage from one state of being to another, each seamlessly joined, he knew not how.

Nor, he thought, was it necessary to know. He was totally incapable of knowing. Only the Creator could know, just as only the painter knows all that goes into the painting or the writer into the writing before it is finally the way he or she intends it to be.

Only the *Work* is important. And once completed and released, it is free, like his daughter, to move forward with its own identity, its own purpose, its own life.

And he still had Work to do.

The elk could wait. His fly rod still lay halfway back down the ridge in the golden leaves that colored the forest floor, his daughter was still away at college, and the stream below still flowed in a temporary form through a temporary world.

And so too, he knew, did he.

– CHAPTER 30 –

OVERNIGHT
SUCCESS

"Terry eased around the north end of the lake on foot
with his fly rod, still casting,
still seeking that one last trout . . ."

The lights floated high and ghostly to the east above the Chama valley, alone and seemingly disconnected from the dark New Mexico night. I had driven north from Santa Fe, through Española and Hernandez and Abiquiu and then high into the Redrock country, through the land of Georgia O'Keeffe and Ansel Adams and Paul Strand, past Ghost Ranch and Pedernal and Echo Canyon and then even higher until finally I crossed the crest of the world and started down the far side.

Despite the pervading darkness I knew what lay unseen all around me, just as I knew the magnificence of the exquisite landscape through which I'd just come beneath the moonless sky. I had flown that sky for over two thousand miles and then driven nearly two hundred more to sleep there among those lights, now hovering high above me between Chama village and the lower rim of the stars. And I knew that soon they would welcome me home to the lodge they surrounded, as they had so many times before.

An hour earlier I had allowed myself the singular indulgence of pausing at *Pedernal*, the grand lady herself, a dark and brooding edifice of igneous stone rising from the high desert, framed by the Milky Way and the millions of stars that soared in one elegant gesture from horizon to horizon. I had stood there praying, alone and unimportant, my arms raised to the midnight sky, magnificently small in my grand insignificance as the universe itself arched overhead.

But now with Pedernal an hour behind me, I turned east up the winding gravel road that climbed nearly two miles from the valley floor to the lights of the lodge. A lone mule deer stood sentry on the front lawn and bolted away as I pulled up to the circular drive and stepped out into the night.

Marianne had left the double front doors unlocked for me, and as I stepped into the greatroom, its silence was welcome and soothing. The dimly lit halls stretched invitingly to the left and right, but I set my single travel bag and camera case down by the door and walked across the room to one of the big chairs that sat in front of the massive stone fireplace and sank into its plushness, feeling the tension of my long flight and drive dissolving into its soft warm leather.

I knew my friends were already asleep down the beckoning halls on either side of me, and that come daylight even more friends would arrive from the Jicarilla Apache Nation to the west, and once more we would all be together in the conference room and around the dining tables discussing the business of the lodge and ranch.

But I also knew that when we were done, there would be a few hours left to head up into the high country with my fly rod.

I was tired, and I knew full well my suite was waiting just down the hall, with the bed already turned down and a small chocolate on my pillow. But for now I reached over and took one of the raisin cakes and the flask of water Marianne had left for me next to the chair, and I awoke just before daylight when Dulce and Miss Sylvia arrived to bring the lodge to life.

It was fine to see my friends again, and the business we did that day was good. We'd all been here together just a month earlier – another long overnight flight, another long day. But I always look forward to these runs west, for I love this land and I love this place, and most of all I love these people. And when we were done, it was time to fish.

As I had come west from Tennessee, so too had Terry Gallagher come east from San Diego. Terry is the ranch's attorney, a true believer, and one fine trout fisherman. On our previous trip, Terry and I had done the same thing we were doing now, grabbing the last few hours of daylight to fish for trout. We'd aimed for Pine Tree Lake, but the rain had left the dirt road there a bottomless mud track and we had been lucky to have gotten out. This time the roads were mercifully dry and so we headed for the high country, first out Willow Creek and past

Sawmill Canyon, then up, up, up until we hit the track that leads to Gary's Lake. The air was cool and crisp, the light crystalline and serene.

The lake sat at the head of a high valley, and at its far end the mountain rose autumn-hued into a cerulean blue sky. At first there were no trout to be seen, but we knew they were here. The evening was calm and undisturbed, and when a pair of mallards flew past my shoulder and out over the water, their mottled forms were just as clearly detailed on its mirror surface as they were in the air. As we followed their reflections out over the lake, there was first one dimple then another, and suddenly a trout cleared the water three times in pursuit of a brilliant blue damsel fly.

Immediately we set up our fly rods, each of us in turn pulling an extended loop of line forward through the guides and tip, then tying on our flies. Terry chose a Michigan Hopper and I a Royal Coachman, and we launched the little boat that we always keep at the lake.

For an hour we fished and for an hour we had no hits. A flock of Merriam's turkeys eased along the trail that edges the east end of the lake. Terry had already changed flies twice, and now I also changed, first to a weighted olive Wooly Bugger and twenty minutes later to a Dave's Hopper.

On my first cast with the hopper, a trout hit. I set the hook, hit him hard, felt his weight and then the involuntary release as the fly flew free. In great frustration I cast back to the same spot, knowingly, uselessly, hopelessly, then picked up the cast and sent the fly sixty feet to the opposite side of the boat. Gentleman that he is, Terry graciously abstained from comment.

The sun was now lowering in the western sky, teasing the tops of the Ponderosas behind us and painting the mountain to the east in deepening shades of scarlet and gold. A bull elk bugled up on the flat to the north. Another bull answered him from the same general direction, then the first bull returned his challenge and suddenly sixty feet away my fly disappeared in a coppery ring reflecting the mountain.

I struck, and this time the hook sank deep and the fly held. The line tore a wicked gash through the lingering light on the surface, and my little Tibor sang sweetly as the line came tight to the reel. For the briefest moment I reached for the drag, but my senses told me it was already set correctly and I withstood the impulse to meddle.

I fully expected the fish to jump as she neared the aspens overhanging the shoreline to the west. But she kept her composure and stayed deep, now turning and throwing a large, building loop in the line as the resistance of the water held it back. I raised my rod high to lift the line from the surface, but when I did, too much of it came free and I nearly lost the tension from the rod tip to the trout, forcing me to strip line in order to reestablish the integrity of the connection.

But the trout was still there in all her strength and elegance, and now she chose to display her grandeur as she leapt high into the evening light. The water flung from her powerful tail reached almost from the nearby aspens to the boat, for Terry had maneuvered us close while I had managed the line. I kept her in the water as she came alongside, declining Terry's offer of help as I reached down and slipped the fly from her jaw. She was still full of vigor and flipped water back at us as she left.

With the sun sinking into the trees and our one trout safely set free, we pulled the boat to shore. Completely gratified with our catch, I took down my travel rod and slid the four sections into the sleeved rod tube and slipped my reel back into its protective case. Then I took my camera and quietly eased into the thick woods in the general direction of the bugling elk whose calls had preceded the trout.

For his part, Terry eased around the north end of the lake on foot, still casting, still seeking that one last trout as I followed the trail the turkeys had come down. The evening was crisp and still, and our voices carried easily across the glassy water; the only interruption was the ubiquitous chatter of the mallards, the impudent songs of the coyotes, the open challenge of the bull elk and finally Terry's clear and confident voice from far across the lake as he called *"hooked up."*

My offer of assistance was at first courteously declined. But four minutes later, with both the fish and the fisherman still at impasse, I began to ease back around the lake in their direction. I picked up my pace, and when I reached Terry I discovered the trout was larger and much stronger than either of us had first thought.

Ditching my camera in the dimming grass, I sprinted back to the boat, but when I returned with the release net, Terry was holding the fish in the water and then handed him off to me as he reached into his vest for his hemostat. As I held the trout, Terry removed the fly and we sent him on his way with our sincere appreciation.

We stood there shoulder to shoulder in the gathering darkness, the only light coming from the dimming mountain and the awakening stars. Once more the coyotes began singing from somewhere out in the night, and again a distant elk shattered the stillness.

We returned to the lodge and a late supper, and the next morning I left for the airport well before daylight just as Terry came wandering down the hall and into the kitchen before heading alone back up into the high country for one last morning in paradise.

Again I paused at Pedernal, this time to watch the sun rise, and I made it to the boarding gate with a few minutes to spare. The jet is now rumbling east beneath me, the captain has just turned on the *Fasten Seatbelts* sign, and I have returned my tray to its upright and locked position.

We are now beginning our descent.

CHAPTER 31

ANGLE OF DECLINE

" . . . the ultimate trout simply does not exist,
unless perhaps it is the first trout or the last trout
of a trout fisher's life. "

'll be a young man someday, but first I must grow old. I must work and wander and then spend huge portions of my life on things that in the end really won't amount to a hill of beans.

I must confront the constraints of space on my body and time on my spirit, for only then can I understand the mistakes I have made in trying to recover that which is not recoverable. And somewhere along the way I must invest the best of what is left in the Eternal.

But I must also make sure that I take occasion to look aside and around and forward and, yes, even back.

And somewhere in the the mix, there must always be trout.

So just what is it about Trout that has become so important to me? Is it the way they have always been interwoven into my life, even before I remember my life? I certainly do not remember my first trout. But I'm sure that Dad never forgot it.

I don't know where it was caught or how it was caught, or the time of day or month of the year or what I had for breakfast that morning. You see, I simply didn't have all that much room for memory back then, for I was far too preoccupied with learning the basics of life and language and growth to be bothered with something so trivial as archiving memories. Now that I think about it, I'm not certain I ever heard the story of my first trout, but the story must surely have been told, for Dad took such things to heart.

It probably happened over on Clear Fork or Wolf Creek or on the Upper Ford of Roaring Fork, or perhaps on one of the other small streams that form the headwaters of the Clinch and Holston, where Dad and I first fished together when he was young and I was new.

And now it seems that the better part of my life has been spent trying to be new again, for I once thought that remaining new was a worthy goal. I didn't realize until much later that even if I *could* become new again, I would just as surely grow old once more.

But now I am at the point in life that being new is not quite as attractive or even as interesting as it once was. Instead, I realize I must seek a sense of timelessness as I approach the Infinite, in spite of the fact that my body is *finite* and carries no lasting hope of its own.

Only a soul can carry hope, only a soul can endure, long after the soul's carrier has returned to the dust from which it came. But for now I am totally incapable of comprehending the dilemma, let alone trying to apprehend the answer.

But I can still wonder about that first trout.

Dad probably had to carry me most of the way in to the stream that day, and I'm sure he held my hand when he set me down and we walked the trail together, him lifting me over windfalls and helping me down banks as I encountered a world still new, at least to me.

I am certain he tied the leader into the black braided line and then extended the old, octagonal metal telescopic rod not nearly full length and baited my hook with a little red earthworm or small minnow or tightly balled-up nugget of bread.

He probably set me on his lap over some particularly compelling pool overhung with laurel and dappled in sunlight, then wrapped his great arms around me from behind, holding my left hand and the line in *his* left hand, and my right hand and the old rod in the other.

And just between you and me, he may even have helped me set the hook when the trout struck.

I'm sure he held onto my belt as I bounced excitedly on his knee, and I know he helped me keep my rod tip up. But I'm sure I did all the reeling and squealing on my own. Well, at least the reeling. And when I had the sinker pulled up tight against the rod tip, we probably swung the trout back into the brush where we then spent a long time on our knees together cleaning the grass and leaves from its sides.

Now, the imagined memory of that fish is far better than the reality, though I do wish I could remember his dance, for I can't recall ever seeing him dance again. It must have been a sight to see, and I'm certain I loved being tossed up and down in the air as our childish giggles filled the autumn woods.

The rest of that day must have been particularly fine for him, with his boy now a real trout fisherman. I may have called for more, or I may have taken a nap on his great coat laid lovingly in the leaves for me as he fished, one woolen arm carefully tossed over my shoulders and one over my legs to keep me warm. I'm sure we fed each other lunch and were back home well before dark, and Mom probably fried fresh trout in her old iron skillets for our supper that very night.

But not *my* trout.

For I suspect that my first trout eventually withered away from freezer burn and its many trips in and out of the cold to be seen and shown, finally to meld into the limitless abyss of a young man's imagination.

And an old man's as well.

And there it permanently resides, along with all the others . . . trout I remember and trout I have forgotten and trout I pray are still to come. And now here I stand, alone in yet another stream, still trying to figure out if one trout is more important than the others.

But I really do not think it possible to answer the question, for God has made each one individually and with great care.

My friend Mike Alberti told me so.

Mike maintains that Trout are the only creatures aside from man that are endowed with such individuality among specimens. My first inclination was to contest the point with him, until it dawned on me that he was right. Mike is a wise and honorable man and is usually right about such things.

We both agreed from the start that the ultimate trout simply does not exist, unless perhaps it is the *first* trout or the *last* trout of a trout fisher's life. Nonetheless, each trout is unique, one of the Master's originals, cast in silver, tinted in gold, patterned by species, unequaled in spirit and etched deeply into the soul of anyone whose life it may touch.

Occasionally a singular trout of exceptional girth or strategy might wrap its jaws around my fly and become one of the more memorable trout I have encountered thus far, and these few individuals become the pegs upon which I hang my entire fishing experience. My most recent trout is always the best, whether or not I actually brought it to hand, if for no other reason than the fact that someday one of these trout will be my last. But for a time in every fisherman's life, their *first* trout is the most important, whether caught as a child or as an adult. So what was that verse again?

> *"Behold, I will send for many fishers,*
> *saith the Lord,*
> *and they shall fish . . . "*
> – Jeremiah 16:16

So does this in some way imply that trout fishing has anything at all to do with religion? Mike and I have discussed this at some length. For my part, I think that perhaps it can, but only if the fishing is not an end in itself. It's just that God has set His trout in such beautiful places and in such beautiful times, as though *Place* and *Time* might actually be real.

But *are* they real?

Or are they relatively simple and artificial matrices that have been given to such relatively simple creatures as ourselves whereby we may at least begin to partially organize and understand our relatively simple lives? After all, we are for now *finite*, as are the trout, and each time we encounter them we are reminded that both *they* and *we* come from the same life source and are therefore part of a greater reality, one that if we can but endeavor to accept and be a part of, then we ourselves may indeed become more.

I suspect it has something to do with a sense of *place*, but nothing to do with *location*. I should never confuse the two. *Place* is not about *location*, for it is not so important *where* you are as it is *how* you are. And when I am casting a fly, I am in a far better place than when I am trolling the world.

Still, it's not entirely about the trout. They are just one vehicle that was given to me long ago through which I might at least *begin* to fathom the Infinite. It could have been golf, it could have been business, it could have been science or music or mirth. It could even have been life itself. But it wasn't.

It was *Trout*.

Certainly I indulged in the others: I once swung a pretty good golf club and was told that my short game in particular had potential. I still run a nice little business in which I do the things I am most aptly suited to do. From time to time I have even managed to squeeze some living into my life and so have on occasion found a temporary sense of place. The problem is, there have been so many of these places, and I have changed them so often that now I have difficulty recognizing most of them as my own.

Except of course for the Trout.

And now I am coming to the cold but certain realization that someday even the trout fishing will fade and become a mere shadow of what it used to be, back when I could move up and down the mountains and streams with ease, regardless of the angle of decline or the complexity of the streambed or even how slippery or moveable the rocks might be; unless I can finally perceive it for what it really was and is and evermore shall be.

Unless I remember the Gift.

Remember the Gift? Remember the *Giver?* Remember the stream that once was mine, where He first planted the seed that grew into me? Do you remember where He first planted *You?*

For this is what I have now become, an aging man who is still a boy at heart, despite his length of years and balance of goods and the trophies and defeats lying strewn like so much chaff in various drawers and files and memories, which for some reason have begun to fade and no longer seem quite so important.

It didn't have to be Trout.

But for me it was, and for that matter it still is, though certainly not nearly so important as being a husband nor so profound as being a dad or a son, although an enormous part of them all.

It has more to do with being a part of the Whole, an intentional *creation* of the *Creator* – an original, just like the trout about which Mr. Alberti speaks so eloquently. Placeless in a world filled with places, timeless along the one-dimensional and one-directional tightrope we perceive as Time, infinite in its beauty and complexity and ability to carry my soul to heights and depths as yet unattained and, for now, just out of reach.

I f trout did not exist and some hot-shot artist painted something that even approximated the hues and patterns of a rainbow or a brown or a brookie or a Rio Grande cutthroat, would it not be interpreted as sheer fantasy, conjured up by an overly imaginative mind surely out of touch with reality?

Yet here they are, these miraculous creatures that we know collectively as *Trout*, each a window into the Infinite, unbound by space, unfettered by time and unlimited by our own limited imaginations.

They already are what we should strive to become: components of the Eternal, integral elements of the greater whole and irrefutable evidence that the Creator is still hard at work restoring and repairing the ruins of a perfect Creation that has been temporarily violated by those who would strive to be a finished painting rather than seeking to be a brush of the Painter.

So let the fishers fish, for He has sent so many of us. But let us never think that we fish for the fish alone. For if we ever fail to perceive the true nature of the Gift, we will just as surely fail to perceive the true nature of the Giver.

CHAPTER 32

FISHING UP EMMAUS WAY

" . . . to this day I am not certain
where he came from, and for
the briefest moment he startled me."

t doesn't much matter where I have been or where I am going; I still can't decide which is the better part of a fly fishing day, the *Going In* or the *Coming Out*. It has, however, become an inescapable truth that the older I get, the more sublime the *Coming Out* seems to grow, for it is increasingly less important what I garnered while I was fishing when compared to what it felt like, what I thought and what I experienced while I was actually there.

Coming Out is the best and most fruitful time to contemplate and digest such things, the best time to process what I have come here to understand in the first place. For if I can't grasp it now while on the outward trail, with the essence of the experience still fresh and full, chances are it will be gone by the time I arrive back at the place where I began.

It has been a long-standing aim for me to try, whenever possible, to begin my fishing by heading *upstream*, if for no other reason than to permit the walk out to be a downhill affair, unencumbered by ever-increasing altitude or diminishing oxygen. And on those rare occasions when I must first descend the trail to begin fishing, the uplifting that I had earlier anticipated at day's end is always just a little more difficult to discern.

My boots are usually well toasted when I am coming out. I especially like walking out on a trail that parallels a new stream, one I have never before fished, a trail I knew was there but did not see as I worked my way upstream during the early hours.

And if as I am coming out, the trail is draped in dusk, so much the better. My fly rod is never heavy at such an hour, and my feet are light and do their work all on their own, leaving my soul to savor the cool, moist air and the whisper of the stream and the myriad impressions of a moment I wish would last just a mile or so more.

And when I have made my way back out to the trailhead, drenched in darkness and trembling time, I turn for a moment and gaze back up the damask trail and wonder what it is and who it is I have left behind.

t was early morning and I was still on my way *In*, fishing upstream below a fogged-in trail on which I had never set foot. To this day I'm not certain where he came from, and for the briefest moment he startled me. But I must confess it wasn't entirely his fault, for I was already preoccupied, in part from the less-than-productive fishing, but mostly from the eight-month project I had just completed, with its many elements still milling about in a cluttered brain.

To be honest, I had no business fishing in the first place with that mindset. But now that I think about it, this is probably exactly why I needed to be there. It had been a full month, a full year, a full life for that matter. Yet there was still so much that must be done. And I still don't know where he came from.

To this day I have trouble putting it all together. At the time I simply realized that he was there with me. No doubt he had been here before; I could tell by the way he eased along the bank and by the old yet perfectly maintained fly rod he carried lightly along with his wading staff, both of which spoke of continued use and expertise. I could see it especially in his gait, which seemed to be ageless. He looked like an older fellow who had somehow stopped aging somewhere in his mid-thirties.

Please, don't ask; that's just the way he looked, and he was vaguely and comfortably familiar when he spoke, though I was absolutely certain I had never laid eyes on him before. But still, I had to wonder.

"Do we know each other? Have we met somewhere?" I knew I didn't know him. But something made me ask. "Are you a guide?"

"Well, sort of . . . "

His voice was smooth and sure, even if his answer was not. " . . . but this morning I'm just fishing."

I liked this guy. I liked his voice, I liked his attitude and I liked the ease with which he was just . . . *there*. I told you, don't ask. That's the way it was. And since the trail now made a great sweeping bend up and away from the creek for a mile or so before crossing it again below the old

Emmaus Road, it seemed I would have some interesting company, at least for a while. And so we talked as we walked. Not about anything in particular at first, until he said, "You seem a little stretched. Hard week?"

"Hard month. Hard *year* for that matter. There's so much to be done, you know. But I did manage to come fishing this morning; you'll have to give me credit for that. But I haven't had much luck, and I've tried just about every pattern in my fly boxes. And this reel . . . "

As I said, it had not been a great morning. Even with all the flies in my fly boxes, I still hadn't been able to find anything on which the trout and I could agree. And now to make matters even worse, my expensive new bench-made fly reel was misbehaving.

"Here, try mine," he said.

"Oh, no thanks, I like using my own equipment . . . you know, pride of ownership and all that." I tried to feign a rather weak, apoplectic chuckle, but I really don't think he bought it for a moment. "Besides, as much as I paid for this outfit, I'd at least like to catch something with it before I head back out."

"Now there's a dangerous pair."

His analysis was not at all accusatory, but it was still a commentary on *something*, and I had to ask, "What? What pair?"

"*Pride* and *Ownership*," he answered. "You have to admit, it does beg the question of who owns who. It's not the gear, it's the living. Here, go ahead, try mine; it's okay." And before I realized it or even thought to take offense, I had taken his rod and reel and he had taken mine, and later after we had fished and eaten and gone our separate ways, I noticed that my new fly reel was working just fine. But I'm getting ahead of myself.

"You been up here before?" I asked as we walked.

"Yup."

"Pretty good place?"

"*Oh yeah.*" He said it with conviction.

Our conversation had already settled into the casual cadence of good friends. I felt comfortable with this stranger without really knowing why or, frankly, even caring. I remember that part, because I am usually not all that forthcoming with someone I've just met. But for now I somehow felt there was something here to gain – not in a selfish way of gaining, but instead an opportunity to learn or even to grow.

I found myself fishing for answers, for questions, for direction, for some place to go with this conversation. I even thought about asking his name, and now I wish I had, just to be sure. But at the time it didn't seem all that important. It really didn't.

And so I asked, "How did you find this place?"

"Oh, I came here to meet a fellow once," he said, "and I've been coming back for years."

"How's the fishing? I haven't done very well this morning."

"Pretty good. I've always done okay."

"What do you fish?"

"Well, it's not so much *what* you fish as *how* you fish. You have all you need there in that vest." He nodded knowingly at my overburdened apparel and its bulging pockets, and I suddenly felt a little self-conscious as I noticed the sparseness of equipment hanging on the leather lanyard that garnished his collar. Still, I couldn't help but wonder how the heck he knew what I had in my vest. Everything I carried, I felt I might need. I had chosen it all quite deliberately and had even taken a couple of things out when I first tried the vest on and felt that it was a tad heavy.

But he did seem to know his stuff, and when the creek finally came back around to meet us he said, "Let's try it here."

The pool was dark and deep and long, reflecting all around and above, but offering little clue as to its depth. It swept away from us just as quickly as it came toward us, and when he offered me his wading staff, I took it without question, though I had never had much use for one before. The old staff was made of a dense but surprisingly light hardwood, and its grip was gnarled but quite smooth and polished from years of use. It was very comforting to lean into as I made my way out into the swift, deepening run. I would never have tried this had I been alone, but with him here to keep watch I felt it would be all right.

"Cast there, to your left," he called from above. And so I did, the bamboo rod unrolling the line out over the water in a perfect, slightly open loop and depositing the fly on its surface with barely a ripple.

The trout that rose to the fly cleared the water by a good two feet. It was the biggest native brookie I had ever seen, nearly eleven inches, a male in full spawning colors. I played the fish quickly so as to either lose him cleanly or bring him swiftly to hand without exhausting him. I felt grateful when I slid my palm beneath his orange-trimmed side and slipped the hook from his jaw as I held him lightly in the water. On the next three casts I caught and released two more.

"They're beautiful!" I called up to my new best friend.

"Yeah, we thought they'd do well when we first put them in here."

"You *stocked* these fish?" I asked incredulously. "I thought they were all natives."

"Well, it's all part of the process," he said. I didn't understand it at the time. I just didn't understand.

"Who's '*we*'?" I asked as I continued casting.

"Oh, my Dad and me. He's the one who set the place up originally and then showed me what to do and how to do it."

"So this is *your* land?" I suddenly felt a little awkward, like I was some place I really should not be. "I thought this was all national forest. It's so far in here. I didn't mean to trespass."

"Oh, don't worry, you're forgiven. We *like* fishermen. Some of my best friends in the world have been fishermen."

There, that was better, though he was just getting warmed up. "But you have to relax."

"What do you mean?" I asked above the whisper of the stream.

"Just what I said . . . *relax*. Let go of the world you're living in. I would bet that your life often feeds upon itself, and that your pleasures and vanities have become an end in themselves . . . and nearly your *own*. I mean, just look all around you. How important is your meeting tomorrow when you compare it with all you see right here and now?"

He did have a valid point, though I didn't remember mentioning anything to him about my Monday morning meeting.

"Look, all this was here before you were ever born, and I guarantee it'll still be here after you are dust. So in the end, none of your worrying will change a thing. Why, I would say you can't even remember the biggest problem you were having this time last month."

Right again, though he was beginning to hit a little closer to home than I would ordinarily tolerate. But he continued. "And that's not all. I mean look as far as you can. Look up. Look around. Look inside yourself. How far can you see?"

"Well, from here I can only see as far as the next pool," I said as I continued casting, eager to move upstream.

"And then what?"

"Uh . . . up to the crest of the ridge there, and then to those hemlocks along the skyline." I surprised myself with my response.

"Okay, that's as far as you can see in *space*; but how about in *time*?"

"Well, for now I just want to see past tomorrow morning's meeting."

"C'mon, surely you can do better than that."

Now I was beginning to feel a little pressured, not at all certain whether I was still the fisherman or had somehow become the fish, and I wasn't sure whether or not I resented it. Still, this guy was taking me places I had never before considered going, but that somehow might bear exploring.

And so I responded, "Okay, I'll bite: I can see all the way to the end of my life, whenever that might be. How's that?"

"Okay, what then," he continued, without any indication of breaking his intellectual stride.

I was beginning to sense down deep that he knew precisely where we were going with this conversation. But for my part, I still didn't have much of a clue.

"What do you mean, *What then?*"

I must confess, I was beginning to bristle a bit. After all, I had come up here to fish and perhaps find some solitude, not to be confronted with a hard dose of logic and reality.

"What then?" His voice was still kind, yet firm and clear and unflinching, and his unavoidable question took me into waters I had not yet plied.

What then?

We fished our way upstream and talked for the rest of the day, I with his gear and he with mine. And though now I can't recall ever seeing him actually land a fish, that evening when I finally left the creek and joined him up on the bank, he had a fire going with four well-seasoned trout laid across a little folding grate, and even hot bread.

There's something sublime about sitting by a fire and eating with a friend, your thoughts and gestures and words mingling and intertwining like the trails of the warm sparks swirling skyward through the cool evening air.

And as we ate and talked and then sat quietly digesting one another's thoughts, I found myself staring into the glowing coals, then following the firelight up through the darkened trees into the starry heavens, and when I looked back, he was heading up the trail with his old bamboo rod and wading staff.

And as I said, the next time I fished, I noticed how smoothly my fly reel was working.

Chapter 33

The Young Man and the Old Fish

"It saddened him to think of what
awaited his brother, upstream above the rapids
and out of sight around the bend, just as it saddened
him to think that both he and this beautiful fish
might perish needlessly."

They lay dying together in the cold wet grass, the Young Man and the Old Fish. Both had traveled great distances to be here, and now both would have been far better off had they not. The fish was barely three days up from open water, here to attend the annual spawning rituals, but the young man had arrived only yesterday, hoping to take advantage of a quick, unexpected break in a self-imposed schedule that had, for all practical purposes, been killing him for years.

It was the young man's fly rod that had brought them together, the great fish ripping wholesale quantities of backing from the singing reel before the man had been able to work his way downriver in perilous pursuit, leaving his brother behind to fight his own thrashing fish. At one point he had stumbled and fallen onto some shallow submerged rocks, and cold water had seeped in over the top of his waders to remind him that he must be very careful.

But he did not want to be careful. Instead, he wanted to thrash about the river as freely as this fish, and for the briefest moment he had resented his humanness. Only now did he notice the sharp pain in his buckled left knee – a small and pitiful ache compared to the bomb that had just detonated in his chest.

He had known for years it would probably happen this way; it had actually taken two heart attacks to kill his father. He just hadn't thought it would happen quite this soon. He was only forty-eight and had intended to get more exercise for years.

Now the young man looked over at the great fish that had killed him, its jaw still enmeshed in the tangled net, pulsing ever slower in the wet grass with each beat of its own heart, desperately gasping for oxygen like himself. He felt sad for the fish, for he'd had no more intention of killing *it* than it had of killing him.

If I could just get him back into the water, he thought. *There's no point in us both dying.*

It struck him as a terribly odd impulse to have at such a pivotal moment in his journey, but still he felt smug in a strange sort of way; for the time being, he was the only one in the world who knew what was happening. It saddened him to think of what awaited his brother, upstream above the rapids and out of sight around the bend, just as it saddened him to think that both he and this beautiful fish might perish needlessly.

But for now he was dying; he was cold and frightened and confused, and he didn't know what he could do, either for himself or for the fish.

He had decided long ago that when his time came to die, he would very much prefer to die alone. He was a private man, and dying seemed to be just about the most private thing a person could do. It wasn't that he didn't want to share it; he simply didn't want to impose it on anyone else, especially someone he loved.

And above all, he'd prayed there wouldn't be strangers.

Now, this was nearly perfect. He was alone with his God and with this fish, and he still had the chance to give the fish back its life, even as God was standing by to receive his.

If only he could somehow manage to get it back into the river.

The tip of his rod lay barely in the water, flirting aimlessly with the thick weeds next to a mink slide. It was an eight-weight Deerfield he had bought from a friend years earlier just for big salmon and steelhead. It had both sensitivity and backbone, something he admired in a finely crafted fly rod. Perhaps if he could reach it, he just might be able to turn the great fish toward the water.

Then if it would simply thrash once or twice, perhaps it could free itself from the net and find the river. And though it may still be hooked, his brother could release it when he found them.

Or would his brother realize he'd already landed the fish?

He might not know he'd intended to release it and so might land it all over again, just for *him*.

There is no time for this! he thought angrily to himself.

At this point, speculation was simply not a luxury he could afford, for he could sense the pain beginning to build once more. Desperately he reached for the rod, but he could grasp only a single loop of line in his chilled fingertips. But still, that might be enough if the drag on the reel was set properly.

At first the line came off the reel without the rod moving. But one clean, hard jerk jarred the whole rig so that he was finally able to reach the blood-stained handle and pull it to him. Only now did he notice that the knuckles on his left hand had been badly scraped on the rocks when he had fallen. But bloody knuckles didn't matter. Nothing seemed broken and his hands still worked, and it was his hands he'd need if he and God were to save this fish.

Gently he lifted the rod tip over the grass to free the tippet. He knew he had to get a good tight line between the rod and the fish if he was going to have any chance of turning it toward the river. But at the same time he had to be careful not to break the frayed leader before he got the fish turned, or all would be lost.

He was still lying on his right arm, and the pain made lifting the rod extremely difficult. But he knew he must discount the pain as he had discounted his battered knee and bloody knuckles.

It was at this precise moment that the old fish convulsed in one final, monumental effort to be free, and with the line already taut and the rod so severely arched, this single movement turned it toward the water and carried it nearly there. But the strain on the worn tippet was simply too much, and it parted with a shock that wrenched the rod from his hand as his entire left side imploded, taking him with it.

H is brother returned to the bend of the river the next morning at first light and slowly picked his way downstream. Finally he reached the mink slide where he sat down to rest.

He desperately needed to be alone. He hadn't slept for nearly twenty-eight hours, not since the alarm had gone off in their motel room the previous morning at 3:30. Now he felt that if he were ever to sleep again, he must first sleep here.

He laid back in the still-flattened grass where he'd found his brother, going on fifteen hours ago. He tried desperately to sleep, but he could not. He still couldn't make sense of it. He sat back up and stared at the old Deerfield, still lying there in the cold, wet grass where he'd spotted it just before he had spotted his brother. He couldn't carry the rod out too and so had left it here, at the time not even thinking about returning for it.

He reached for the handle but had to turn onto his side to get it, finally picking it up by the tangled line and pulling it to him. The drag was set correctly but the tippet was broken and the fly was gone. His brother was much too good to break a new tippet. He puzzled for a moment before he realized what was missing – his brother's landing net was nowhere to be seen. He stood and began feathering the tall, dripping grass with his hands, and there in the edge of the water he saw the tangled mesh and the worn bentwood frame of the net they had carried for years.

And as he picked it up, he understood.

There were little flecks of silver scales still embedded in the mesh, and when he knelt to examine the grass more closely he found a few more scales among the breadloaf stones that lined the water's edge.

This explained the broken tippet; he had stood beside his brother as he'd tied on this tippet just a few minutes before they had both hooked their individual fish.

He stood, stepped up to where he'd left the rod, picked it up and settled back into the cold wet grass, a weak smile crimping his dampened face.

When he awoke he was better, and for the first time in many hours he actually felt hungry. He reached into his coat pocket and fished out the half-eaten oatmeal cake his brother had handed him yesterday morning and finished it.

He stepped down to the water's edge and knelt, lifting a palm full of cold water to his salty lips and face. Then he picked up the old fly rod and net, raised them to the river for one long moment and turned to go.

CHAPTER 34

THE MEETING
UPSTREAM

" . . . it seemed to hang there
in front of him for a much longer moment
than yesterday evening's fish . . . "

They had planned this trip for years.

"If I get there before you do, look for me upstream."

That was the plan, for they both knew that their chances of actually arriving there at the same time were extremely slim. You know how it is. And in the end, it turned out they were right.

Still, when he got word that his father had left without him, he couldn't help but feel let down, though he had known all along that with the differences in their timing and schedules, it might work out this way. And when it finally came time for *him* to leave, it came rather suddenly and unexpectedly, and he wasn't sure of the route to take or which path to follow once he got there. But he knew it would be all right and that he would understand when he arrived, for the trail would not be hard to discern.

It never had been hard, this trail that had always been laid out clear and unrepentant for him, this trail he'd always known he could trust.

They'd done this many times before, he and his Dad, back in the world they both knew so well – whoever reached the stream first knew the signs to leave for the other to follow, signs no one else would have ever recognized, but which for these two stood out like blue lanterns in a moonless night. And sure enough, when he finally left his vehicle and his vision adjusted to the dim light, the signs were clear enough. And he was thankful.

The journey here had been long and much harder than he'd ever imagined it would be, and there had been times when he'd been hopelessly lost. Nights are long when you are lost, and if it hadn't been for the directions his Dad had given him back in the world, he knew he might never have gotten here at all.

Now he headed upstream, just as they had previously agreed, straight into the soft, early-morning light, its glare not nearly so intense as to distort his vision, but a bright enough path that he felt certain would lead him where he needed to be.

It was lovely water, by far the best he'd ever seen, and he had already seen the best. The riffles appeared golden, and the pools were deep and inviting, and when he knelt to drink from the stream it was as though the water itself were alive. And for the first time in a long time, he *too* felt alive. Really *alive*. And suddenly, all he had ever possessed, all he had ever desired, all he had ever been counted not in the least, and all that mattered was where he was and where he was going and the path laid clear in front of him.

He peered into the soft morning light, its intensity growing as he made his way upstream, searching both for that which he knew and for that which he had not yet encountered.

And then he saw it, a rise unlike any he'd ever seen, a broad arrow-shaped head thrust out of the water to inhale who-knows-what, and that great arching back and dorsal fin that slowly and deliberately followed as it curved back into the depths.

Future and Past were now totally meaningless, and the Present was all that mattered. And even though he had no idea what the trout had just taken, he immediately cast the same fly he'd been casting yesterday evening when he had been called away, and it suddenly disappeared in a massive swirl.

He struck on sight, and the fish burrowed deep, as though she had planned this from the beginning. Amazingly, it looked and behaved very much like yesterday's fish; only this one was larger and more powerful, its sides deep and rich, as though it were cast from pure living gold.

This fish, too, vaulted high into the air, though it seemed to hang there in front of him for a much longer moment than yesterday evening's fish before heading over and back into the current. He tried to get below it, but he was already at the tail end of the pool and the water fell steeply from where he now stood, so that even if he could have somehow gotten back downstream, he could never have played the fish from there.

And so they simply danced in place, he in the edge of the current and the great fish deep and even with him, and it seemed they might dance there forever. Until he heard the voice.

"Who's playing who?"

It was a good voice to hear. And as he looked up and over his shoulder, he saw the face he'd come here to find, coming down to meet him, and it was a good face to see. It had been too long since he'd seen that face and heard that voice, and for the briefest moment the great fish no longer mattered and he would have laid his fly rod down right then and there, fish and all, and run up to embrace the hand that had so patiently awaited him. But he was brought back to himself by an old familiar question, a question he had heard many times before and was now glad to hear again:

"What can we do to help you?"

"We? Who's 'we'?"

Only then did he notice that there were actually two of them, and the other fellow did look somewhat familiar, and he suddenly recalled that they had met once on another stream in another time. But just then, the fish turned, not downstream as he had feared, but upstream into the flow, and as he moved up to meet it, his companions moved down to join him.

They all four arrived at the same place at the same time, he and the fish still in the water and his two companions looking down as he eased it out onto the golden shore beside them. And as he knelt in the light-laden stream and rinsed the gold dust from the great trout's sides before releasing her, gathering angels anxiously hovered overhead among the treetops bathed in the warm morning glow, and his Dad and his Lord waited patiently there above him and smiled.

And when he stood, they welcomed him home.